Jesus and I are Friends

The Life and Ministry
of
J.R. Miller

Faithfully

J R Miller

Jesus and I are Friends

The Life and Ministry
of
J.R. Miller

JOHN T. FARIS

SOLID GROUND CHRISTIAN BOOKS
Birmingham, Alabama USA

SOLID GROUND CHRISTIAN BOOKS
2090 Columbiana Rd., Suite 2000
Birmingham, AL 35216
(205) 443-0311
sgcb@charter.net
http://solid-ground-books.com

JESUS AND I ARE FRIENDS:
The Life and Ministry of J.R. Miller

by John T. Faris (1871-1949)

First published in 1912 by Hodder & Stoughton, NY City, NY

SGCB Classic Reprints

ISBN: 1-932474-68-4

Cover Design by Borgo Design, Tuscaloosa, Alabama
Contact them by e-mail at nelbrown@comcast.net

Manufactured in the United States of America

FOREWORD

Dr. Miller was too much occupied with things deemed by him more important to give any attention to the selection and putting aside of material concerning his life. He was so busy writing and speaking and living and loving, with the shaping of the lives of others in view, that he took no time to think of the world's interest in his life. It never occurred to him that there would be any demand for the story of his life, and he discouraged the efforts of friends who sought to gather material for a biography.

Yet Dr. Miller was the author of the truest possible description of himself. He did not think of it as a description—in giving it he was only telling the reality of his faith in his Master. But all who knew him agree that the description was true and accurate. He said, "Jesus and I are friends." This is the story of the life of Dr. J. R. Miller, told in five words.

Dr. Miller gave glimpses of his life in his books. Whenever he wrote to others of things they should do from day to day, he was telling unconsciously of

things he was doing himself. This fact is apparent
from the brief quotations from his writings on the
page facing the beginning of each chapter in this
volume. These quotations, taken together, help to
fill out his own descriptive statement: " Jesus and
I are friends."

J. T. F.

PHILADELPHIA, September, 1912.

CONTENTS

ILLUSTRATIONS

ANCESTRY AND EARLY YEARS

An honoured parentage is a good heritage. It puts one under tremendous responsibility, too, for its blessings are a sacred trust which must be kept unsullied, and accounted for. To be unfaithful in such circumstances is not only to leave our work undone, but to mar, possibly destroy, the good work of others which had been put into their hands to finish.—*From "Morning Thoughts for Every Day in the Year."*

The Master sets before us the goal of our being. He has a beautiful plan for each life. There is something definite for which he has made us, into which he would fashion us, and toward which all his guidance, education and training will tend. This is not a world of chance—it is our Father's world. All the experiences of our lives have their part in making us what Christ would have us become, in bringing out the possibilities that he sees in us when we first come to him.—*From "What Christ's Friendship Means," in "The Beauty of Self-Control."*

CHAPTER I

ANCESTRY AND EARLY YEARS

(1840 to 1862)

JAMES RUSSELL MILLER was always too much engrossed in the service of God and men to pay any attention to collecting facts concerning his ancestors. But those who have had the opportunity to trace the Miller family to its source across the sea, have learned facts both interesting and illuminating.

The ancestors on the mother's side were named McCarrell. The McCarrells came originally from Scotland, where Sir Lachlan McCarrell—the chief of the clan—was a friend and companion of Sir William Wallace. Early in the seventeenth century the McCarrells went for religious freedom to Ireland. In Ulster they found the blessings they sought. Samuel McCarrell, one of the descendants of the transplanted Scotchmen, died in County Armagh in 1789, at the age of ninety-five. His son, Thomas—the great-grandfather of J. R. Miller—was born in County Armagh in 1741. He learned the trade of a weaver, and later came to America in 1777, in a merchant ship commanded by his uncle. The blockading of the ports pre-

vented his immediate return home. Soon he had
no desire to return: his heart was so stirred by
what he had seen and heard of the struggles of
the Colonies that he became a soldier of the Revo-
lution about October, 1777. He was with George
Washington in the camp at Valley Forge the following winter. He had with him his Bible and
his Confession of Faith, which are treasured to-
day by his descendants.* It is a tradition among
these descendants that he was once struck in the
breast by a bullet, but that the Bible saved his
life.

During the first years after the close of the war
the young Scotch-Irishman lived in Virginia. In
1789, with his wife and three children, he took the
hard journey across the mountains to Washington
County, Pennsylvania. Two of the children were
carried in the ends of a pack thrown across the
back of a horse; the third was held by his
mother as she sat on her horse. In 1811 Mr.
McCarrell bought the farm " Pleasant Hill,"
near Eldersville, which is still in the possession

---

*On the title page of his Confession of Faith is this inscription:

THOMAS McCARRELL, HIS BOOK

God give him grace therein to look
That so he may the truth contain,
And these improve while life remains.

Lest some should find the owner's name
Or if he lose and you should find,
I pray you to restore again.

THOMAS McCARRELL, 1774.

of the family. He was a Ruling Elder in the "Seceder" Church now known as the Cross Creek United Presbyterian Church. The members of this godly household frequently made the trip of sixteen miles to Canonsburg to attend service. He died March 29, 1836, at the age of ninety-five. His wife, Eleanor Rusk Mc-Carrell, died at the same age, on September 19, 1846. Surviving them were five children—three daughters and two sons. Four of these married and founded Christian homes, in which the family altar was always maintained. From two of these homes and the homes that succeeded them, came seven ministers of the gospel, whose combined service has been more than two hundred and fifty years.

Mary McCarrell, who was born November 21, 1782, married Robert Creswell. Their daughter Eleanor married James Alexander Miller, whose great grandfather, Samuel Miller,—also of Scotch-Irish descent—was born in 1717. Samuel Miller's home was near Hickory, in Washington County, Pennsylvania. Here he spent most of his life. In 1794 the headquarters of General Lee in the campaign to suppress the Whisky Insurrection were at his house. His son James—the third of his eleven children—moved in 1798 to a farm near Tomlinson Run Church in Beaver County. In 1812—when ninety-five years of age—Samuel Miller rode on horseback from the Washington County home to the Beaver County farm. The distance—thirty

miles—was made in a single day, with a rest at
noon for dinner. He lived seven years after this
memorable trip, dying in 1819 at the age of one
hundred and two. In his last will and testament
this godly man provided funds for the purchase
of a Bible to be given to each of his grandsons.
He felt that he could make them no better
bequest.

James Miller married Polly Russell. Their son,
James Alexander Miller, married Eleanor Creswell. Ten children blessed their home—three sons
and seven daughters. One son and two daughters
died in infancy. Both of the surviving sons became ministers of the gospel. James Russell
Miller was the second child, though his older sister
died before he was born, on March 20, 1840.

In 1840 the family home was near Frankfort
Springs, Pennsylvania, on the banks of the Big
Traverse, a merry little mill stream, which drains
one of the most beautiful valleys in the southern
part of Beaver County. The old homestead and
the mill, where the father spent his days labouring for the support of the family, are still
standing.

The home on the Big Traverse was a house of
prayer. When it was founded the family altar
was set up, and it was never suffered to be broken
down. As the children came into the home they
soon learned that whatever else of the household
routine was omitted, family worship was never
forgotten, and never slighted. Neither pressure

of business nor the presence of guests was ever offered as excuse for the omission of morning and evening Bible reading and prayer. The family worship took time: the hurried repetition of a verse of Scripture and a sentence prayer was never considered enough; but there was invariably the reverent and devout singing of a Psalm, the reading of a chapter from the Bible, in regular course, and a prayer in which the members of the family were committed to God's keeping, and the interests of the kingdom of God, at home and abroad, were remembered. It is recalled by one who often participated in these sacred services that a petition seldom omitted pleaded that the love of God might be shed abroad in the hearts of the kneeling suppliants,—"that love which works by faith, which purifies the heart, which overcomes the world." For a long time the one who tells of the petition wondered where in the Bible it could be found, until diligent search showed him that it is a mosaic from the words of Paul and Peter and John. The priest at that family altar was a Bible student.

He was also a man of prayer who knew how to point out to the family the way to the Throne of Grace, because he had found it himself and was travelling it daily. He knew the meaning of the exhortation, "Pray without ceasing." One of the burdens of his private prayers was that his boys might become ministers of the gospel. It had been his wish to become a minister, but the way was closed—the claims of his dependent parents on his time could not be passed by. After the death of their first-born, the husband and wife promised God that if a son was given them, he should be dedicated to the ministry.

In this godly home the Sabbath was sacredly set apart. Seldom, if ever, was the family pew empty, though the church was several miles distant, and the roads were frequently well-nigh impassable. There were no evening services in the churches in those days, but the home became a little sanctuary. The devout father was the minister. Matthew Henry's "Commentary" was taken from the shelf, and his exposition of the text of the evening was read aloud. Then came the reciting of the Shorter Catechism; as the children grew old enough they were required to learn this as rapidly as possible. Each took part in the recitation as far as the questions had been learned, and read the answers which had not yet been memorised. When all the children had completed the one hundred and seven answers, no catechism was ever seen at the Sabbath evening service. The father would propose the first question, which was answered by the one sitting nearest to him. This one would become questioner in turn, while the one answering the second question would propose the third in order, and so on to the end of the series. The method required the memorising of both questions and answers, but those who mastered the book in this way had a working knowledge of theology that served them excellently in later life. Every member of the family felt as James did when he said in later years, " I owe to my father's home the religious training which has meant so much to me in my life."

The home in which religion was given such prominent and constant place was not the abode of gloom. The children were glad to spend the evening in the company of their parents. Music was their solace during many of these evenings. James frequently took part in this relaxation, either with his rich tenor voice or on the violin. Frequently there would be a guest in the family circle, for not many days passed without the coming of one or more visitors. Frequently on Sunday a minister who had come to assist the pastor at the communion service or on some other occasion would be entertained by Elder Miller. The conversation of these visitors did much to shape James's purpose in life.

A visitor to the neighbourhood of an entirely different sort left an indelible impression on the mind of the growing boy. When he was an old man he said of this visitor:

" Sixty years ago a man went through Western Pennsylvania, making infidel or atheistic speeches. He had some eloquence and spoke persuasively, and many men's minds were poisoned by his words. Some years later he met Christ and surrendered to Him, becoming an earnest believer and a zealous Christian. One of the earliest recollections of my boyhood is of this man holding meetings around my home and speaking boldly for Christ. When he became a Christian he saw his terrible error in having laboured so against Christ. He saw that he had done great harm to many lives by his arguments against Christianity, against the Bible, against God. And he went to the same neighbourhoods, where he had sown seeds of infidelity, and spoke in the same halls and schoolhouses, trying to undo the evil work of his earlier years. Very pathetic was the sight of the old man at his unavailing work."

The picture of the vain efforts of this old man to undo the evil work of his earlier years was afterwards to point the warning that evil words once spoken are gone beyond recall.

Mr. and Mrs. Miller were a blessing in the homes of others as well as in their own family circle. Seldom was there sickness or sorrow in a neighbour's house when one or both of them did not go at once on an errand of mercy. Their readiness to help in this way soon made an impression on James, who was noted when quite young for that eagerness to go to houses where there was sickness, which was a characteristic to the end of his life. Neighbours of early days lovingly tell of his ministry to a large family, all of whom were stricken with typhoid fever; for weeks he gave himself to the care of the household, till all but two were nursed back to health. The father and one son died. After these deaths the volunteer nurse

—then a student away from home—made frequent visits of sympathy to the bereaved family.

With his sisters James attended the district school in Hanover Township, where he learned the elements of a fair English education. That he was an eager student was testified by an early teacher, Wallace Wilson, who died only a few months before his pupil of those early days. He said it was always a pleasure to teach James Russell Miller, and he took particular delight in telling of the ambitious student's request that algebra might be added to the curriculum. The teacher frankly confessed that he knew nothing of the subject, and proposed that both should study it together. The old man's eyes kindled as he recounted the success of that winter. With the unassuming spirit for which he always was noted, his pupil aided him in understanding the new branch of learning.

When James was about fourteen years old, his father moved to a farm near Calcutta, Ohio. In the new home James was popular among his schoolmates, as he had been in his Pennsylvania home. The young people of the neighbourhood delighted to gather at the Miller fireside to enjoy one of the evenings of good-fellowship for which the household was noted. It is easy to understand this when the lovable James had lively sisters, one of whom he described in fascinating manner in a letter to a friend, written years after he went out into the world:

" Your letters always remind me of a little sister at home whose wicked pranks are never to be forgotten, and whose letters always come filled with little bits of wit and sarcasm. She delighted always in teasing me when I was at home, in continually playing tricks with my letters, hiding my books and papers, and otherwise endlessly annoying me—but always with such good humour, and with such a quiet, innocent air, that, no matter how evil-disposed, I could not for the world get angry with her. However, she knows very well that her big brother is very good-natured and never apt to grow angry, and, moreover, that he enjoys teasing quite as well as she does. She is a good girl, and next to my mother the dearest on earth to me. I like spirit and have a particular fondness for a style of intercourse which some very punctilious and exact people call impudence."

The writer of this letter was looked up to as a leader by the members of the household and by his boy friends from other homes. A younger companion was deeply impressed by his earnestness of purpose and his integrity of character. In a letter written years later this companion said:

" You have been a constant uplift to me all my days. You know that naturally I was a shiftless creature. My only ambition in the early days of my existence was for a broomstick horse. Your example and gentle influence did much to wake me up, and it has been a mighty inspiration to me ever since. If my life has been of any service to the world, this is owing to God's blessing on your life.''

One day James chiselled his name most neatly on a great stone near the Calcutta home. The companion just mentioned saw the letters and carved his initials beneath those of the one whom he desired to imitate. Other boys followed his example, leaving their initials on the stone, not always with the same neatness and skill, but in a way that showed the power of example. That stone, with its silent testimony to the influence of one earnest youth on his companions, may still be seen by visitors.

For three years after going to Calcutta James attended a district school during the short winter months and worked on the farm during the summer. Many of his evenings were spent in private study. Thus, in 1857, he was well prepared for entering Beaver Academy in his native county.

In a letter written in 1911 to Daniel W. Fisher, D.D., concerning Calvin W. Mateer, D.D., long a missionary in China, he said:

'' Dr. Mateer was my first teacher in Latin and Greek. I never can forget how he received me when I first went to the academy at Beaver. I was a bashful country boy, full of enthusiasm and eager to learn, but knowing almost nothing. There was no room ready for me in the academy the first night, and the young principal took me into his own room and into his own bed. The impression he made upon me that night, especially at the time of prayer before we went to bed, is one I never shall lose from memory.''

At once he became known as a good student. It was not long before he was asked to assist in teaching some of the lower classes in the academy. Later he taught also in the Beaver Female Seminary. Always he was diligent and painstaking in the performance of his double duties as student and tutor.

Rev. J. A. McGill, then principal of the academy, was still living when his pupil-teacher of those days closed his life on earth, and he wrote this testimony:

'' Mr. Miller gave himself heartily to everything that was for the good of the academy. He was a diligent student, a genial companion, a trustworthy friend.''

He was not content to study merely to make recitations and pass examinations, but he inspired those he taught with a like spirit. He not only thoroughly mastered the subject in hand, but so far as his time would permit he made himself familiar with the general literature that came within his reach. The poets were his great delight, and his mind and soul were enriched by many of their treasures. He seldom attempted to phrase his own thoughts in rime, yet all that he wrote revealed the true spirit of the poet. It was his habit to try to reproduce from memory sentences and paragraphs which had impressed him, thus making them his own. Then he would write original sentences and paragraphs modelled on those of the masters. He was a painstaking composer, often making many drafts of his compositions, until they reached as nearly as possible the high standard which he set for himself. His ideal was simplicity and purity of diction, and he was fond of illustrations that would be like windows through which the visions of the soul might become real to others.

Yet he took equal delight in studying the book of Nature which was spread out so entrancingly before him. Those who are familiar with the scenery of the Ohio Valley, especially in the vicinity of Beaver, know that no praise of its beauty can be called extravagant. In the autumn season especially, the fields and forests of that region present a wealth of beauty. Long walks in the country and extended rowing excursions on the river increased his love for God and God's world and all mankind.

Busy as he was—in preparation for recitation, in hearing his own classes, in athletic interests— he had time for the ministry to others for which he was always known. A daughter of Matthew Duff, an assistant in the school, wrote in the summer of 1912:

"I have heard both father and mother speak of the way J. R. Miller had of doing little kindnesses that boys are not in the habit of doing. One such kindness was taking care of me one night when I was a very sick baby and my parents were worn out. . . . It has been my habit for years to read to mother from Dr. Miller's ' Year Book.' I don't think she ever realised that he had grown old.''

Very early in life he had begun to manifest a deep interest in vital personal religion, and this was intensified during the first winter at the academy. Those who were his fellow students speak of him as a young man of prayer. He was a regular and devout worshipper in the church, where his voice joined heartily in leading its service of praise. He despised ostentation in religion, yet religion was to him a matter of daily life, and it shone out in every word and deed. One has said, '' His life was a happy illustration of the Master's promise, ' He that believeth on me, from within him shall flow rivers of living water.' ''

He made no parade of the fact that his fullness of life came from God, yet his intimate relations with God could not be hidden. His associates knew that his life was renewed by daily contact with Him whom, even then, he was fond of calling his Friend.

On October 10, 1857, he united with the Associate Presbyterian Church of West Union, located near Calcutta. As the Associate Reformed Church was one of the bodies which formed the United Presbyterian Church—on May 26, 1858—he was from that date a United Presbyterian.

Thereafter, whenever the young Christian was at home, he took his turn in leading family prayers. The younger members of the household gladly accepted him as assistant, for they realised his sincerity and earnestness of purpose. Already they knew him as a prince in prayer. One of the distinct recollections of his sisters is that he was much given to secret prayer. One sister has told of his coming home one evening after the family had retired, bringing with him a friend who was to share his room for the night. Before retiring he stepped into the room where two of his sisters slept, and, supposing them to be asleep, knelt in prayer. As she saw his countenance in the moonlight it seemed to be like the face of an angel. She was only a child, but she felt that the humble room was the very gate of heaven, for he who knelt by her bedside was holding converse with the Father.

His brother, too, recalls vividly how, when James would go to bed after spending an evening in study, he would pray long and earnestly. James thought his brother was asleep and he gave himself without reserve to his prayers. He would frequently kneel for an hour at a time, and would whisper as if talking to a friend. "He didn't talk about his religion," the brother has said, "but he made it very real to me when he gave me a Bible in which he wrote this message:

"'Read this Book as a letter from the dearest of all friends.'"

There was no trace of the I-am-holier-than-thou spirit. He was as simple in his bearing when a boy as he was when a man. There was a deep, genuine sympathy in his heart that made all he met feel at once he was their friend who understood them and in whom they could confide. He was free from that patronising air which too often impairs the influence of those who would be helpful to others. Those who worked beside him in the harvest field or met him in the neighbourhood social gatherings, as well as those who were his schoolmates, agreed that he was one of themselves, who showed in every word and action that he was interested in them and wanted to be of use to them. So, as he advanced gradually beyond the companions of the home, no jealousy was aroused, but on all sides there was rejoicing.

During his academy course he taught one term of school at Industry, Pennsylvania, and another at Calcutta, Ohio. So he did not enter Westminster College at New Wilmington, Pennsylvania, until 1861. He was so far advanced, however, that he was graduated in June, 1862. In the autumn of that year he entered the theological seminary of the United Presbyterian Church at Allegheny, Pennsylvania.

Throughout the first year at the seminary his mind was full of the war. He longed to enlist. But he had almost completed the year before his course was interrupted by military service.

WITH THE CHRISTIAN COMMISSION

We should not be content to let a single day pass in which we do not speak some gracious word or do a kindness that will add to the happiness, the hope, or the courage and strength of another life. Such ministries of love will redeem our days of toil and struggle from dreariness and earthliness, and make them radiant in God's eye and in the record they make for eternity.—*From "Upper Currents."*

We represent Christ wherever we go. He is not here to-day in human form, but He sends us in His place. We are to act for Him, speak the words of kindness we would speak if He were here, do the deed of love He would do if He were in our place. We must be faithful to our mission. We must never be silent when we ought to speak. We must never speak when we ought to be silent.—*From " Witnesses for Christ," in " A Heart Garden."*

CHAPTER II

WITH THE CHRISTIAN COMMISSION

(March, 1863, to Sept. 19, 1864)

MR. MILLER was in college when Fort Sumter fell and the country was plunged into the throes of civil war. He had just reached his majority, and like ho-ts of other young men, felt the patriotic impulse to offer his life at once for his country's defence. Some months passed, however, before his enlistment, and then circumstances prevented his serving in the ranks, as it was his earnest purpose to do. He enlisted as a member of a company recruited in and about Calcutta, Ohio. The company left for Camp Dennison, near Cincinnati, Ohio, where they were encamped for a time. Their enlistment was on the condition that they were to be placed in a regiment as a company. At that time, however, there was no place where they could be so attached, and the only way the officials in the department could accept them was as individuals, to fill vacancies in other companies. This was not in accord with the wish of the young men, and they returned to their homes. In the meantime Mr. Miller continued his studies until he saw the opportunity for effective service through the new Christian Commission, which was organised soon after the disastrous Battle of Bull Run.

During the early months of the Civil War the Young Men's Christian Association of Washington and New York and the Tract Society of New York and Boston sought to give help both temporal and spiritual to the soldiers. The work was too great, however, for the handful of workers which these agencies could put in the field. So the National Committee of the Young Men's Christian Association called a convention which met in New York City November 14, 1861, to consider the needs of the army. The work of the United States Christian Commission was outlined and the organisation completed next day. Twelve members were named who were to carry out the purpose of the convention. George H. Stuart of Philadelphia was made chairman of the new organisation, which began its work at once, with the hearty endorsement of President Lincoln, the Secretary of War, the commanding general, and others in authority.

The work of the Commission, as outlined at the convention, was both special and general. The official records of the body defined the activities thus:

" The relief and care of the wounded, during and immediately after battle, and meeting the wants of men in such places as parole and convalescent camp, and other emergencies, may be called ' Special Work.'

" The supply of religious service in aid of chaplains, or in their place, for hospitals and regiments without chaplains, the supply of reading matter to men in hospitals and throughout the army, the distribution of bodily comforts, and the promotion of intercourse with home, may be called ' General Work.' "

The work was done by voluntary and paid delegates, under the direction of Field Agents. Each agent had charge of one army corps, and directed the activities of from five to ten or more delegates. General Field Agents supervised the Field Agents. In all 191 delegates were commissioned in 1862; 1,067 in 1863; 1,880 in 1864; and 934 in 1865. Many of these served from four to six weeks only, but a large number were active for much longer terms. The average number at work in 1862 was 48; in 1863, 115; in 1864, 217; in 1865, 310.

The work was supported by gifts of money, clothing, printed matter, food and comforts from all parts of the North. Many gifts came from abroad. The total value of gifts of all kinds administered during the war was more than six million dollars.

A statement made by General Grant concerning the work of the Christian Commission at the final meeting of the representatives in Washington City, February 11, 1866, indicates its great value to the country:

" By the agency of the Commission much suffering has been saved on almost every battle field and in every hospital during the war. No doubt thousands of persons now living attribute their recovery, in great part, to volunteer agencies sent to the field and hospitals by the free contributions of our loyal citizens. The United States Sanitary Commission and the United States Christian Commission have been the principal agencies in collecting and distributing these contributions. To them the army feel the same gratitude that the loyal public feel for the services rendered by the army."

Equally strong and hearty was the testimony of General Meade on the same occasion:

" One of the brightest pages in the history of the great war from which we have just emerged will be the record of the noble spirit displayed by our people, in their devotion to the wants and comforts of our soldiers. No one not in the field and witnessing the scenes of distress there exhibited, can fully appreciate the services thus rendered to humanity. The United States Christian Commission was conspicuous in the great work of love and charity, and I am sure that the survivors of the war will, like myself, ever have in grateful memory the debt of gratitude so greatly due to it."

It was in March, 1863, when Mr. Miller—then a middler at Allegheny Seminary—began his service as delegate. He promised to serve for six weeks. But his work was so well done that at the expiration of this period he was urged to remain for the summer campaign. A good situation was waiting for him at home, but he determined to give this up and stay where he felt he was needed more. He was, therefore, assigned to the Army of the Potomac. As Assistant Field Agent, it fell to him, together with two others, to direct the extensive operations of the Commission at Gettysburg after the notable battle fought in July of that year. The Annals of the Commission contain this reference to the service there rendered:

" Every station occupied by the Commission on this field of blood is worthy of a special record. Suffice it to say that at every point of this field, as at others of like character, the effort to relieve temporal wants was blended with Christian counsel and consolation, and as ever before, so here, the Holy Spirit attended such ministrations with the divine blessing."

The following extract from a letter written by Mr. Miller a few weeks after the battle of Gettysburg gives an insight into the character of the work in which he was engaged:

" General Meade and staff were at the service last Sabbath morning. Two of his staff are known to be religious men, and take part in religious services, I have noticed, and Captain P. of General Meade's staff remarked the same to me, that there is a marked change in the observance of the Sabbath around headquarters during the past month. Every Sabbath grows stiller and quieter.

I was at headquarters last Sabbath morning. It was the calmest and most like the Sabbath of any I have spent in this army. I blessed God for it. Flags were down, offices were closed, and none but the most important business was transacted. General Patrick called at our tent, conversed for a half hour, inquired concerning arrangements of service during the day, selected some books, papers, etc., and then attended services himself, morning and afternoon. He says: ' We have just got what we want. We have talked the matter (of having service at headquarters) over many times, and have made efforts to have this end accomplished. Burnside tried it, and sent off for ministers, but the services never succeeded in awakening interest. Now we have the very thing we want, and we mean to keep it. Soldiers are becoming most deeply interested themselves at all our stations, and I believe that we have never had so much encouragement to work.' "

Several weeks after this letter was written an attack of typhoid fever was brought on by his tireless labours, and Mr. Miller lay for some time in the hospital at Washington. The only hint of this illness in the notebook kept by him during the campaign with the Commission is given thus:

" A sweet little Scotch girl came every day into my chamber with a bunch of flowers, or a cup of nice tea, or a whole miniature tray of delicacies for me, or—if nothing else—always with a sweet smile on her face, a look of encouragement and cheer, and a tender, sympathising word. I always longed for her coming, and believe that she did more to cure me than my physician. Her sweet, winning ways were made doubly so by her native Scotch manners, her broad accent, her captivating frankness, and her choice little delicacies. I shall always remember that gentle tap on my chamber door, after a stealthy, velvet-slippered pit-a-pat through the hall, and then the slow, quiet opening of the door, and the little face with bright, sparkling eyes, and smiling lips peeping in, as if half fearful to enter, and then the tiny little creature with the gifts of flowers or luxuries from the table, gliding up to my bedside. Ah, what is dearer than a sweet child! I love the simple prattle and the innocent mirth and the unaffected frankness of a child.''

Soon after leaving the hospital, on October 25, 1865, Mr. Miller was appointed General Field Agent, and was assigned to the Army of the Cumberland. He wrote in his journal:

'' I left Pittsburgh November 10 to take charge of my field, and, stopping for a few days in Cincinnati to make arrangements for my work, I passed on to Crab Orchard, Kentucky. Here transportation was wanting, and the remainder of the way had to be made on foot. It was still one hundred and sixty miles to Knoxville, over a mountain road of terrible muddiness, and one which was in many places next to impassable. I started, however, and reached Barboursville only to learn that Knoxville was besieged, and that my further progress was stopped. Waiting there a few days I passed on to Cumberland Gap, delayed there a week, and reached Knoxville at last on December 10, one month after leaving Pittsburgh.''

On December 15, 1863, he wrote further of his activities:

'' I find in the city at present about seventeen hundred sick and wounded. All the hotels, churches and other public buildings, besides several private dwellings, are occupied as hospitals. I have visited most of these and find there conditions as good as could be expected under the circumstances, but there is still a great want of sufficient food and clothing. The army, during and before the siege, made such demands upon the subsistence of the country, that the citizens cannot do much. I trust we shall be able to bring these gallant fellows many of the comforts of home. They are worthy, and will not be forgotten by the kind and generous ones who are working for the soldiers.''

In January, 1864, he wrote:

'' The opening of the month found me on a Tennessee river steamboat at Chattanooga, awaiting its departure to return to my field. I had with me a small supply of stores and a delegate, Rev. William Gaston, of East Liverpool, Ohio. . . . Our boat was without accommodations, and we found ourselves poorly prepared to endure the violent storms and most bitter cold of many years. We left Chattanooga on New Year's evening, and reached London Sabbath morning.''

Next day he reached Knoxville, where he opened rooms and commenced distribution of the scanty supplies available.

On January 18, Mr. Gaston left for home, his term of service having expired, and Mr. Miller was alone for a week.

" I felt discouraged. Day after day closed with a heavy heart and an unsatisfied spirit. On Sabbath morning my heart was gladdened by the reception of a telegram from London, stating that stores and two delegates would reach Knoxville by the evening train. Never was news more welcome. My heart was rejoiced and my hopes brightened. The train came and brought two ministerial delegates. . . .

" Early in the month I made application for a church which I found unoccupied, intending to have it fitted up as a soldiers' chapel. It was a Methodist church, formerly, and was occupied by the congregation till the time of the siege. Then it was taken in some irregular way as barracks, and when again left vacant after the siege, was in a terribly filthy condition. On the 26th I obtained permission to fit it up as a chapel, and incidentally got a squad of prisoners and went to work at cleaning it. By Sabbath I had it in tolerably good condition, and on Sabbath morning (31st) it was opened for divine service and rededicated to God. The attendance was respectful and encouraging. . . . A daily prayer meeting was appointed at 1:30 P.M. each day."

The work during February was sadly interrupted by the departure of delegates who had served their appointed time, and the arrival of others to take their places. But Mr. Miller knew how to inspire green workers. Within a few days after the arrival of delegates from the North, they were, in most cases, doing effective work. This month a new department of activity became popular with the soldiers:

" In our room a writing table sufficient to accommodate twenty or thirty men has been fitted up, and paper, envelopes, pens and ink constantly supplied. From one hundred and twenty-five to two hundred letters are written daily. In our reading room files are kept of the Pittsburgh, Cincinnati, Louisville, Nashville and New York dailies, besides the magazines and miscellaneous periodicals. No one can realise the value and importance of these facilities to the soldiers till he has some experience of the privation of army life. . . . Our rooms are always crowded."

On March 1 a station was opened at London, not far from Knoxville. A humorous incident of the work there was included in the journal:

" The room assigned to us for a reading room had been previously used by a band of minstrels for a concert room. When we took possession of it, they erected their tents close by, and carried on their performances. For several nights they had some success, but soon their former crowds diminished till the concerts were almost deserted. The reason was that our religious meetings in the church attracted all. After a week or so, the proprietor came into the Commission rooms one morning and said: ' We can't run these things together. Your prayer meeting is drawing away all my patrons.' ' Well, which do you think is the

more profitable, the prayer meetings or your performances?' he was asked. ' I like the fifty cents
mighty well,' he replied. . . . However, after
one other trial he left the town, and donated his
lumber, etc., to the Commission.''

On April 15, after directing the opening of several of the stations, and the advance of delegates
with supplies to the front, Mr. Miller left Knoxville, expecting to spend some weeks at home in
preparation for licensure at the June meeting of
his Presbytery. After Presbytery it was his purpose to visit the churches in the North, present-
ing the work of the Christian Commission and
soliciting financial aid. One of the delegates at
Knoxville wrote of him:

'' He leaves behind him a warm host of friends,
whose unanimous testimony is that he faithfully
discharged the many and laborious duties that de-
volved upon him. The high estimation in which
he is held here is well expressed in the words of
George, the coloured cook, who says, ' Massa
Miller am a gemman, ebery inch of him, from the
crown ob his head to the sole ob his feet.' ''

In his journal Mr. Miller told something of the
difficulties of war-time travel:

'' I took the cars to Chattanooga and the train
ran off the track near Athens, and we were all
tumbled head over heels, so that it was a marvel
anyone escaped. As it was, however, none were
killed, though fifteen soldiers were injured; but
I escaped unhurt. I reached Chattanooga at mid-

night, and pressed on toward Nashville the same
night. We took the Alabama road, via Decatur
and Athens, thence north to Nashville. Stopped
a few hours in Nashville, then moved northward.
Train soon broke down again, and we lay all
night near Bowling Green. In the morning we
were tied on behind a freight train and pulled
along to Cave City. Here we stopped for the purpose of visiting Mammoth Cave. . . . We spent
the night partly in the cave, and returned to Cave
City Hotel in time for the train. Then we pushed
forward for Louisville, where we arrived before
night. . . . Next day at noon we took steamer
for Cincinnati. . . . Went to church in the morning, to Sabbath school in the afternoon, and
preaching again in the evening. . . . On Tues-
day I started eastward.

"I had scarcely reached Pittsburgh, however,
when I was telegraphed for, to proceed to headquarters at once, to assume direction of the work
in General Butler's Department. Thus all my
fond anticipations were blighted, and I went away
to the field again. The Pittsburgh Committee
made a most strenuous effort to have the order
countermanded, but to no effect. I must go, and
at once. I reported accordingly in Philadelphia
on April 25, and left after a few hours' consulta-
tion for Baltimore and Fortress Monroe."

Then began some of the most important work
of Mr. Miller's service. He was sent to the front
with the Army of the Potomac. He directed the
delegates—who were now available in large numbers—for service in camp, on the field of battle,
and in the hospital. A station was established

very early in May at Bermuda Hundred. This
was for work in General Butler's army. There
were two hospitals here, and a number of batteries
without chaplains. At Point of Rocks, four miles
up the Appomatox, a hospital was erected which
remained throughout the war. From Bermuda
Hundred, the wounded of Sheridan's Cavalry
were visited, and large quantities of stores distributed to them. When the Eighteenth Infantry
went to White Horse Landing, Mr. Miller and
his corps of delegates accompanied them, estab-
lishing the station which did so much to relieve
the wounded.

A vivid paragraph was written at Cold Har-
bour, where fifteen thousand men were cut down
in fifteen minutes:

" Our delegates all went to work at once, and
that right earnestly. I divided them off into several companies. One company was to carry water
and wood, and keep up fires, another to prepare
cornstarch, soup, lemonade, etc., another to carry
these articles to the men, another to write letters
and converse with the dying. And thus the work
began and went on during the whole day. The
next day was Sabbath, and it came upon the earth
in all its beauty and sacredness. I rose early.
The sun was just above the horizon, and the first
beams of morning were still struggling through
the trees. The birds were singing sweetly, the
air was moist and dewy, and everything was still
and hushed, as it used to be at home on the blessed
Sabbath. For once the deadly instruments of war
were hushed, and it seemed like a Sabbath morn

of peace. But a few rods from where I stood lay some two thousand mangled men, suffering, some of them dying, while almost at my feet was a big open trench, and at its edge lay eight or ten dead bodies ready for interment. Soon the shrill crack of the pickets' rifle bursts on my ear, the cannon thunders off at the left, and all the illusions of a moment since are dispelled. It is still Sabbath morn, but a Sabbath morn of blood. And it rises upon us in the midst of a bloody battle field, with carnage, death and war all around.

" Monday afternoon, June 6, we had a brisk shelling. The villainous things shrieked and exploded over us and all around us. It was hot enough for an old soldier, and went rather roughly with certain newer ones. Two batteries were opened in the spot occupied by our hospital—one hurled its shot and shell from the right, another from the left. It was a serious enough matter that afternoon, but now in my quiet I can see the ridiculousness of some of the scenes I beheld. A chaplain had been stopping with us since we pitched there and had been quite sick, unable to leave his cot of fir boughs under our flag. As soon as the shells began to whiz and burst around our tent, he straightway brightened up, for the time forgetting his sickness, and was soon *en route* for a distant part of the woods where safety might be found. In his haste he left his coat and valuable books and papers. Next day he returned, but his memories were still vivid, and he tarried but briefly, saying nothing about being sick.

" All our delegates but one left for parts unknown. The woods soon covered their line of retreat, and shut them away from danger. After the shelling had ceased they gathered back to the tent one by one, till all but two returned. Their stories were amusing. Two positively affirmed that they had no regard for themselves, but they felt bound to seek their safety on account and for the sake of their wives and children. One or two confessed frankly that they did not like to be shot at, and deemed discretion the better part of valour. Only one had courage enough to stay with me till morning, while all the rest went back two miles to another camp hospital. When morning came two went straight to White Horse, resolved to find a place where they could be free from the terrible scorching of rebel shells. A tall rock on the crest of the hill had to shield a number of boys from real or supposed danger. They formed a line for twenty or thirty yards behind it, and just as the direction of the coming shell seemed to them, so they shifted. When a shell came from the right, the whole pendulumlike column swung to the left, and *vice versa.*"

Delegates and stores reached City Point June 15. A station was at once established which existed for more than a year. Here some of the most strenuous work of the campaign was carried on by the Commission. Mr. Miller was active here as well as at Point of Rocks. Of his work at the latter place he wrote, under date of August 31, 1864, a report that gives a splendid glimpse of the activities at a busy station.

" There are now about two thousand patients in the hospital. Our establishment here consists of one chapel tent for storeroom, one chapel flag for sleeping tent, one for religious services, one wall tent for warehouse and one for office. I have only eight delegates at present, though I should have at least ten. Here is my mode of work in the corps and hospitals. Early in the morning six or seven delegates go in a two-horse wagon to the front, carrying with them a good quantity of reading matter and hospital stores,—for every regiment has a number of patients in its regimental hospital. These delegates all spend the whole forenoon in one or two brigades, taking the troops in their order on the line. They aim to see every man as they go, and either give him something or speak a kind word to him. This ' front ' work I deem very important, even when we have the hospital work, and I have always aimed to keep it up as regularly as practicable.

" We have dinner at half-past twelve. From noon till half-past two are resting hours. From half-past two till half-past five they spend in the hospital. Each delegate has four or five wards. During this visit no services are held. The delegate passes through his wards, speaking a word to every man, and relieving his wants, as far as possible, but making the visit as far as practicable a pastoral one. After tea, he holds a brief religious service in each ward, and this closes the day's labours. The work goes on thus from day to day, and a more delightful success could not be expected. All the delegates are in the best of spirits, and all are hard workers. At night all are weary, and sleep is welcome, but morning finds all refreshed, and ready and anxious to begin a new day's labours. At the front, on this part of the line, there is no picket firing, so that we can visit every part of the line safely, and see the men at their work. This adds greatly to our work, and enables us to make it complete and thorough. It is my aim to have every regiment visited at least once each week."

The campaign closed for Mr. Miller in September, when he was made General Field Agent in the Shenandoah.   He reached his new field September 19, the day the Battle of Winchester was fought. There, in the midst of the wounded and dying, the young Field Agent entered the final stages of his services for the Christian Commission.

AT THE FRONT

A very little love for our neighbour wrought out in a bit of everyday kindness is worth a great deal of talk about love which finds no expression in act.—*From " Letting God In," in " Finding the Way."*

Fill the day with love. Forget yourself and think of others. If there is a call for kindness, show the kindness now, to-day; it may be too late to-morrow. If a heart hungers for a word of appreciation, of commendation, of cheer, of encouragement, say the word to-day. The trouble with too many people is that they fill the day with neglects, with postponements, with omissions, with idle words and idle silence. We do not realise vividly enough that there are many things which if not done to-day need not be done at all. If we have slept through the hours when duty waited, we may as well then sleep on.—*From " Guarding Our Trust," in " A Heart Garden."*

CHAPTER III

AT THE FRONT

(Sept. 19, 1864, to April 1, 1865)

FROM the beginning of his work in the Christian Commission, Field Agent Miller did his best to persuade the delegates to leave with him full records of their work. He even prepared a large notebook, on the cover of which he wrote the request:

" Delegates will please note all incidents of their work in this book. Also full reports before leaving."

In a few instances the request was observed, but evidently most of the men were too weary when they felt free to seek their rough beds to do anything but go to sleep. The book devoted to them would have been sadly neglected but for Mr. Miller's own observation and reports. He was as weary as the delegates when night came—probably more weary, for during his service in the army he was as unceasingly active as in his later life. Yet he would remain at his table hours after others were sleeping, writing his story. On November 16, 1869, he said:

"Nearly midnight, and around me thickly packed in layers on the floor the rest of the 'family' are sleeping, while I have been drudging all night through piles of letters, stereotyped business sheets, trying to get square with life and my work. As the finale I wrote a long letter to *mon cher ami* Crammond Kennedy, away in Scotland. I was to have gone with him over the water, had not the meshes of duty to my country and humanity so entangled me that I could not escape from the army."

In these records, written while others slept, it is noteworthy that he gave full credit to the delegates, speaking of them in the highest terms if he could, passing over their faults and failures without a word when this was possible, and making excuses for them when it was necessary to make some reference to their shortcomings. Perhaps the bitterest comment he permitted himself concerning a delegate was written after trying experiences with "a very bright and fascinating young man, who has occupied a full-sized delegate's place in bed and boarding houses, but who has not done very much of a delegate's work . . . one of two young gentlemen, who look for all the world like a flower pot. He had a pretty face, a fine coat, a clean shirt, polished boots, smoothly combed hair, a bewitching smile, a graceful bow, a smooth tongue, a neat hand, a gentle voice, and was altogether decidedly Frenchy, artistic." Then followed a sentence in which Mr. Miller, who was already showing the passion for service that later made him so remarkable, revealed his attitude to life, " But I always liked the bee better than the butterfly." This is the only reference in his notes to such a butterfly; there was too much to be said of the bees in his reports.

The monthly reports of the activities of his department were made up from the daily records. These reports are accurate and complete. A number of them are quoted in the records of the Christian Commission. The largest of those thus selected for preservation was written at the close of his first quarter's service with the Army of the Shenandoah. Those who would read a vivid story of the work at the front of the heroes of the Commission should study this document as it is given in the full in the volume of annual reports of the organisation. Generous portions are quoted here, not only because of the glimpses they give of Mr. Miller's work in the last year of the war, but also because they clearly reveal so much of the ripening character of the thoughtful, diligent, humble writer.

The paper is dated at Harper's Ferry, December 30, 1864, and begins:

" I have the honour to submit the following report of the operations of the Christian Commission in this field, from the organisation of the department, in September, till the close of the year. The impossibility of keeping full records during the hurried work of organising, while an active campaign was in progress, will account for any deficiencies in the first part of my report.''

After speaking of his arrival at Sandy Hook, Maryland, on September 19, he says:

'' Both difficulties and dangers attended the forwarding of supplies and delegates to the field for the sufferers at Winchester. The railroad from Harper's Ferry to Winchester was destroyed. Guerrillas infested the country in search of plunder. We had to hire poor wagons and teams, until good ones could be purchased and sent to us. The difficulties were overcome, the dangers did not stop us. Our wagons, supplies and delegates were hastened forward, and reached the front in safety.

'' Arriving at Winchester, a room was secured, where the stores were deposited, while the wagons went back immediately for more supplies. In two days we again went forward with two wagonloads of choicest hospital stores, and with a reënforcement of ten delegates. This second supply I accompanied myself. I at once visited all the hospitals, and reported to all the different surgeons in charge that we had a band of workers who had come to do their part in caring for the brave sufferers. In every instance the proffered aid was gratefully accepted. To many of these officers, as well as to their men, the Christian Commission was almost unknown. The Sixth Corps had served long in the Potomac army, and, of course, had met the Commission in every camp and field since its organisation. But the Nineteenth Corps had known but little of our operations previously to this campaign. And the Eighth Corps, having been serving in the mountains of West Virginia mainly, knew but little of us. However, every facility was granted us, and with no ceremony, our ten delegates, fresh from home, and anxious to do all in their power to alleviate suffering, went to work. Since that time, we have had a great and uninterrupted work at Winchester.

" The battle of September 19th was a most important one. Previously to the campaign that so auspiciously opened with this engagement, the Valley of the Shenandoah had indeed been our ' valley of humiliation.' There we had suffered defeat after defeat, and the brave men who had fallen on many disastrous battle fields, lay scattered over every portion of the valley. But the 19th was a new day in the history of our military operations in this section. Instead of constant and disastrous defeat, we now entered on a series of as brilliant successes as have marked the history of any army of similar power and strength since the war began. Morning saw the enemy, proud, defiant, and confident,—night found him routed, reduced in numbers by many thousands, flying in disorder, leaving the machinery of war, and the débris of battle scattered all along his path. The victory was complete, overwhelming, and destructive; and the news that went to the world thrilled loyal hearts everywhere with joy. But victory always costs something; always leaves sad wrecks behind; amid the shouts of the victors on the field are heard the groans and wails of the dying; and with the rejoicings at home over the news of victory, there are always mingled the throbs of saddened hearts; for loved ones fall on every field of strife, and every battle sends sadness and desolation to many homes.

" The battle of the 19th was bloody. Hundreds of brave men fell to rise no more, and several

thousands were wounded. The sufferings for
many days were very great. In addition to our
own wounded, there were two thousand of the
enemy's wounded left in our hands. These were
collected in distinct hospitals, with their own surgeons and nurses; yet they demanded care at our
hands, on the principle—'If thine enemy hunger,
feed him; if he thirst, give him to drink.' The
great number of friends that these rebel wounded
have in the city of Winchester and the scarcity of
the friends of the Union made it certain that as
far as help from citizens was concerned, the rebels
would fare much better than our own men, and on
this account I directed that the principal efforts
of our delegates, at the first, should be on behalf
of our own men. However, one delegate was appointed to visit the rebel hospitals daily, to supply
them with reading matter, Testaments, papers,
etc., and in cases adjudged really needful, to supply also small quantities of hospital stores.

" The scene presented after the battle was truly
a heart-rending one. Winchester was literally one
vast hospital. All the churches and other public
buildings were filled; while almost every private
house had its quota of wounded and bleeding soldiers. There have been but few times since the
war began when there was greater need of ex-
ternal relief. There was nothing left in the country; the government supplies were all back; the
nearest base was Harper's Ferry, over thirty
miles distant; and the intervening country was
overrun with guerrillas, so that nothing could go
forward safely, unless under the protection of a
strong military escort. I cannot pass over this
period without bearing testimony to the noble
and self-sacrificing labours of the loyal ladies of
Winchester. When they saw the brave defenders

HEADQUARTERS IN THE FIELD
(*Mr. Miller seated on the chest, at the left.*)

of the old flag, which they still so dearly loved, stricken down in the streets of their city, they at once entered on their work of mercy, and ceased not till all the brave men were made comfortable. They shared their last morsel with them; they washed, and dressed, and cheered the weary sufferers, and bent over the dying to catch their last whispered message to dear ones far away. There are a few names in Winchester which will go down into history garlanded with honours, and coupled with deeds of heroism and magnanimity.

" The world will never know the nature, value, or importance of the work performed in the hospitals by our delegates. It was a quiet, unostentatious work of mercy. Entering on their labours there in a time of greatest suffering, they worked by day and by night among the wounded thousands, washing, dressing, feeding, praying with the dying, burying the dead, and calling upon the living to repent and be saved. It is now nearly three months and a half since the work began, but it is not yet ended. During this time, five hundred men have died in these hospitals; several thousand have been transferred to other hospitals; while several hundred still remain.

" As soon as the railroad was restored, Martinsburg became a place of great importance to our work. Almost every wagon train from the front brought down two, three, or five hundred men on their way to the hospitals of Baltimore and other cities. During the first few weeks, these men were taken, as soon as they arrived, into the churches and other public buildings, from the wagons, and there remained till the following afternoon. It is twenty-two miles from Winchester to Martinsburg. And over all this distance, in hard army wagons, over rough roads, with no beds, or even straw to lie upon, and with no rest, and nothing to eat by the way, these poor, mangled men had to travel. We were always apprised of their coming an hour or more before they began to arrive, and large camp-kettles full of water were placed over the fire, and soon forty or fifty gallons of tea were ready. Then, with tea, crackers, cheese, meats and fruits, our delegates hurried about from place to place, till all were fed. Then came the bathing, and washing, and dressing, and it was usually well-nigh morning before all was done; but after a night's hard labour our delegates have always felt amply repaid for their toil in the gratitude of many noble hearts. In the morning the same routine began again; and at noon the brave fellows were placed in the cars for another long, hard ride; and our last act was always to make them as comfortable as possible on their hard beds on the cars.

" Too much cannot be said in praise of the noble ladies of Martinsburg, and their deeds of benevolence performed toward our suffering soldiers during the campaign. The many men who have from time to time lain in the hospitals of Martinsburg will always remember with gratitude the loyal people who so gladly and so freely shared with them the comforts and luxuries of their own homes.

" During the campaign the twofold object of the Christian Commission has been kept steadily in view. While caring for the body, and labouring to alleviate bodily sufferings, we have aimed to lose no opportunity to speak a word for Jesus. We have always borne in mind that our soldiers are beings for immortality; and, in going from cot to cot, among thousands, our delegates have not failed to remind them, if but by a hastily

spoken word, that they have interests far higher
than those of time. Prayer meetings and other
brief religious services have been regularly held
in all our hospitals; and a quiet, but powerful,
work of grace has been constantly moving forward.

" The only station of the Commission in operation, in the department, at the opening of the campaign, was the one at Sandy Hook. To-day we
are represented at Sandy Hook, Harper's Ferry,
Martinsburg, Cumberland, Beverly, Stevenson's
Station, Winchester, and at the front, four miles
south of Winchester. At that time we had but
two delegates in the field. During the campaign
over eighty have been enrolled, who, with few ex-
ceptions, have laboured faithfully and diligently
in the service of our Master."

The admirable report closes with this paragraph:

" Our plans for the winter contemplate the erec-
tion of chapels in every camp, so that all may have
an opportunity to hear the gospel; the establishment of libraries in reach of all who desire to
read; the organisation of prayer meetings; and
the distribution of Testaments, papers, books,
tracts, etc., everywhere. The field is ready and in-
viting, the harvest promises to be plenteous, and
we ask for the reapers. Many thousands who now
ask for the Word of life, in one year hence will
sleep quietly beneath the sod. The time for work
is now. We ask for grace to begin the new year
with renewed zeal, and to enable us to do more in
the future than in the past."

An editor of the Pittsburgh *Gazette* visited Harper's Ferry in February, 1865. In his leading

editorial on February 13, after speaking of the workers, he said:

" The General Field Agent is Mr. J. R. Miller, of the United Presbyterian Church, a man of indefatigable industry and fine administrative abilities. A nobler or more generous man we never met; and if we were to relate even what fell under our observation of his deeds of substantial kindness to all around him, but especially to a bereaved and sorrow-stricken woman, and at serious expense to himself, our language would be thought extravagant.

" The headquarters is a decent ' shanty ' containing three rooms and a little kitchen. There they live and labour and hold their nightly meetings for religious worship. The soldiers are always coming and going, and here they congregate every evening to sing and pray, and discuss their joys or sorrows. Here they often linger to talk or sing together of those better things which only true believers realise and understand. . . . During the present winter hundreds of soldiers have become earnest Christian men at Harper's Ferry and in the camp around. Even the delegates themselves are astonished and delighted at the progress of the work. But it is not more than might be expected; for probably nothing has been so much like the work of the great Master himself as this work of which we are speaking."

Always extremely modest and unassuming, Mr. Miller said nothing of his part in persuading the soldiers about him to give themselves to Christ. But it is certain that God used his untiring, sympathetic, prayerful efforts in the salvation of hundreds. Between the lines of the Field Agent's reports and private records one can read hints that tell how he was serving his apprenticeship for the work of later years, that was to be so marvellously blessed. Once he sorrowfully wrote a record of failure that tells how earnest he was in seeking the lost:

" I talked to a man in the hospital and urged him to accept the Saviour's gracious offer of pardon. ' No,' said he, ' I have lived a most sinful life for thirty-five years, and have always refused a Saviour's love. I know what you tell of Christ is true. I know that I shall suffer eternal punishment, yet I do not repent; but, sir, I am too brave a man to come now at the last hour and beg for pardon. It is cowardice that drives men to Christ when they are going to die. They seek salvation just when—and not till—they find that they cannot live in sin any longer. No, I will die as I have lived.' And nothing could overcome his determination. Before morning his spirit had flown."

With what joy he turned from a record like that to a letter to the secretary of the Christian Commission, in which he said:

" Again we have to thank God for another month of prosperity and success. Everywhere his Spirit has been preached and his glory advanced in the salvation of souls. Such a great outpouring of the Spirit amid the rude and ghastly scenes of war, imparts a new and holy light to the cause for which we are struggling."

In this letter workers were mentioned by name, and much is said of their success as winners of souls. Of himself, as the leader of the work, he said nothing, although in the last paragraph he revealed his agency in inspiring the workers in the only true way:

"I have always believed that the secret of the greatest success of preaching the gospel in the army is in the fact that the gospel only is preached. We have no time nor opportunity for pulpit embellishments. Men are taught their true condition, and told of the only Saviour. The personal conversation, the earnest prayer meeting, the brief and simple sermon, and the Bible lesson are the means which God sees fit to bless."

Thus in the closing month of the war Mr. Miller's time and thought were largely taken up with the problems to which he was to devote his life—the problems of the hearts of men.

IN CAMP AND HOSPITAL

Christ is our Friend. That means everything we need. No want can be unsupplied. No sorrow can be uncomforted. No evil can overmaster us. For time and eternity we are safe. It will not be the streets of gold, and the gates of pearl, and the river and the trees, that will make heaven for us—it will be the companionship, the friendship of Christ. . . . The consciousness that Christ is our Friend and we are His should check every evil thought, quell every bitter feeling, sweeten every emotion, and make all our life holy, true and heavenly.—*From " Christ and I Are Friends," in " The Book of Comfort."*

How are we to find what our place in the universe is, and what we ought to do with our life? Does anyone know, and can anyone show us, but He whose we are, who has made us and planned us for our course? We see at once that if we leave God out of our life, ignore Him, fail to recognise Him as our Master, seek no direction and guidance from Him, we can only wreck our career. The only ambition in life that is wise and safe is the ambition to be what God made us to be, to do what God sent us into the world to do, to fulfill the divine purpose for our life. And it follows that only Christ can guide us in choosing our place and our work. —*From " This One Thing I Do," in " A Heart Garden."*

CHAPTER IV

IN CAMP AND HOSPITAL

(To September, 1865)

MR. MILLER's notes of his life at the front tell of many letters and visits from anxious mothers and other relatives who sought information of wounded soldiers. It was one of his greatest pleasures to do what he could for these inquirers. Once he wrote:

" I have never felt happier than to-day when receiving the blessings of a dear old Scotch woman, who came here to seek her son. We have in this office a list of all the patients in the Winchester hospitals, and then we take a list of all who pass through from there on their way to Baltimore and other hospitals. We found that he had passed through two days since. She heaped blessings on our heads for our kindness to her boy, for we had fed him on his way through. Leaving some gifts for her other boy to be forwarded to him—he is well and at the front—she turned her feet to find the wounded son."

Thus the writer revealed his eagerness to minister to the sorrowing that was so characteristic to the end of his life. Another characteristic—

his ardent love for children—was shown when he wrote:

" The soldiers who have lain in the hospitals at Martinsburg will never forget the sweet little girl with the blue eyes and chestnut curls who, every day, stole noiselessly to their cot, having in her hand some little dainty, and on her sweet face a smile of welcome. She is not more than eleven or twelve, but womanly beyond her years, and possessing a heart large enough and good enough for a Florence Nightingale. Up bright and early in the first golden beams of morning, and with her hands laden with the little luxuries of home, away she trips lightly, gayly to the hospital. She hastens noiselessly around through the rooms, stopping at the side of every weary sufferer, asking him how he rested, and how he feels this morning, and leaving here and there some delicate morsel. When she has finished her morning's work, away she goes to school, but no sooner are her duties over there than off she glides again to repeat her morning's work, and again at evening she bears cheer and comfort to many a drooping heart. She is tender-hearted, and often drops a tear over some poor sufferer, to see how sorely he is pained, and as he tells her of his home, and the dear friends whom he will never see again. She was passing through a ward with us one morning when we came to a man whose sufferings were most agonising, and whose face was already paling before the approach of death. It would have been a heart of stone that could have looked unmoved on that scene. The dear child laid her face in her hands as the great tears flowed from her eyes. When we had left the hospital she looked up through her still weeping eyes and said,

' I was not a baby to cry when I saw that poor man, was I ? ' "

After reading this passage, one is not surprised to find this also:

" Somehow I can never get over my foolish weakness of falling in love with little girls. Blue eyes, chestnut curls, rosy cheeks, neat dress, sweet smiles, and kind winning manners in a little girl of ten or twelve are not to be withstood. . . . Little girls can do more by the sweetness and in- nocence of their free young hearts to allay troubled spirits and to cheer and soothe in the hour of suffering than most of those who are older. There is a purity and a sincerity and a simplicity in their manners and words that captivates hearts."

He had a prophetic insight into his own future when he said, a little later:

" I have always felt that by the peculiar traits and talents which God has given me I am able to do more for the instruction and culture of children than many men who have different capabilities. I have laboured much among children, and I have in many instances been able to soften the rudest, to tame the wildest, and to overcome the wilful- ness of the most stubborn. And all, too, by the sweet, gentle, winning power of kindness.

" Last Sabbath I met for the first time a dozen little boys and girls in my own room, and organ- ised them into a Sunday school. To-day we met there again. There were several new ones, and the interest is certainly very great. During the past week the little girls have been almost wild with enthusiasm. . . . They hang around me like children over a parent, or sisters around a brother.''

The man who could minister so tenderly to children was capable of the heartiest sympathy with the woes of older people, as was evident from the very next record in the journal:

'' Five men were sentenced to be shot to-day for the crime of desertion. Wednesday afternoon, while waiting on the platform for the train going eastward, my attention was directed to two ladies also waiting for the train. One of these was very old and frail, with tottering step, bowed head, and time-silvered hair. Her eyes were sore with weeping, and a swift glance told me that some great burden was resting on her heart. The other was young, evidently a daughter of the elder lady, with a face sober and thoughtful, and while she stood her eyes wandered listlessly and absent-mindedly upon the scenes around. A commonplace inquiry on the part of the younger lady opened a conversation between us, and on the way to Relay House I had frequent conversation with her. She told me of her mission to Harper's Ferry. Her brother was one of the number to be shot that day. The old lady was his mother. His father was an old man of nearly eighty, too frail to leave his room, and both parents were evidently near death. Eleven weeks ago her brother left home without telling anyone of his intentions. No tidings came of him till last Friday morning, when the telegraph bore the sad message: ' Father, I am in prison here, sentenced to be shot the 17th. Am not guilty of desertion as they say.

Can't you do something to save me?' The father could not leave his chamber, but the heartbroken mother and sister hurried forward at once to Washington, and by an interview with the President had the sentence suspended. Then they came to Harper's Ferry to see the boy. They saw him twice, and then hurried forward again to Washington, on which journey I met them. . . .

"Before the hour appointed for execution all but two of the convicted men had been respited. The execution of the sentence on the remaining three was suspended. The hour came, however, and the two for whom there seemed now no hope of mercy were borne off to the appointed place, and all the solemn preparations were enacted. In a few minutes more, or perhaps only seconds, the ill-fated men would have been launched into eternity. But just at the last moment, when their hands were pinioned and preparations were making for the sentence, an orderly dashed up on horseback with an order to stop the execution of the sentence. The orderly had ridden with all possible speed. His horse had fallen in the road and was able to go no farther. He seized another horse and dashed on, waving the paper in his hands, that they might see him coming, lest he should be too late. He was just in time, and the poor men yet lived.''

Little wonder if amid such scenes the young worker was sometimes cast down. His heart was continually going out to the sufferers about him, and vitality was so exhausted that he could not always be cheerful. He was careful not to tell others of his depression—he was never willing to be a discourager. The pages of his journal only were told the secret, and they did not betray him. On August 8, 1864, he wrote:

" How these gloomy hours weigh me down! I know it is wrong to be gloomy. I have no right to walk under dark clouds while over all the sun is shining. I know I should always be cheerful and bright and happy. God makes us to enjoy life, and he desires us to be happy. The general tenor of my life is even and bright. Fortune favours. I have won for myself a high position among those who labour for the temporal and spiritual welfare of our soldiers. All seems to be moving well, and I should be happy at all times.

" Yet at times, in spite of my strongest efforts, I feel the shadow of a cloud, as it steals over me. A sigh or two, a few hours of despondency, a sleepless night, a useless day, and then all is bright again. Life is a strange medley, a check-ered pathway indeed, streaked with light and draped in gloom. Especially in the army is life liable to its hours of darkness. How I long at times for the quiet, the leisure, the enjoyments, the privileges, the love of home! I was brooding the last hour over the wrecks, the sad home-wrecks, the heart-wrecks, the wrecks of pleasure and of joy, that the war has made. I was think-ing of the happy hours of three and four years ago, of the happy friends with whom I mingled. I was thinking of my dear associates. I remember as if it were but yesterday the walks, the talks, the tender words of love, the calm, cheering words of counsel and encouragement. I had my dark hours then, my hours of discouragement and some-times almost despair. I had my rivals and my enemies. . . . I had my anxieties and cares, for I have borne my share of responsibilities. Per-

haps few so young have had more. And I often
felt the burdens resting upon me, crushing me
almost to earth. . . .

" To-night I have none to whom to bear my sorrows. There is no human being that listens to
my words of discouragement, no tongue to whisper
words of cheer, no heart to love, no heart to receive my aching head. I am a stranger far from
home. I am sad to-night. I have been looking
on society rent and torn by the ravages of war.
My friends of boyhood, my associates of past
years, my fellows in Latin and Greek, are nearly
all gone. The enemy's balls have laid them low."

The entry that makes this record worth its place
in this biography follows immediately afterwards.
It tells of the triumph of the strong faith of the
lonely helper of the soldiers as he wrote in triumph:

" Jesus is my friend, and why then languish in
vain for earthly comforters? Christ alone is true
and sure—Jesus Christ my all shall be."

The reader can see the strong man throwing
off his discouragements, squaring his broad shoul-
ders, and rising with new courage to face the burdens of his life of ministry.

It was by daily, hourly communion with his
Friend that he gained strength for his tasks. And
the knowledge that others were praying for him
cheered him.

" As I have knelt late at night in my tent, to
praise God for his goodness and invoke still longer

the sunshine of his favour, I have always felt that
I was not alone. I have felt that far-away loved
ones were—possibly at that very moment—bow-
ing like myself in prayer. I have known that for
me a voice of prayer arose to him who answers.
I have felt stronger in heart and stronger in faith.
I bless God for the privilege of prayer, and
doubly, when it becomes the electric chain that
binds heart to heart, and all to heaven.''

And again he wrote:

'' Gradually the clouds of war are lifting, and
rays of glorious light are bursting upon us. May
we not hope that the end is near, and that when
this terrible tragedy is over, our land may never
again be called to witness such scenes of suffering and strife? The only fitting posture for the
Christian in these days of blood and heart-wrecks
and home-wrecks is on his knees. Let us never
cease to beseech God to have mercy on us, and to
take away His sore judgments from us. ' The
sacrifices of God are a broken spirit: a broken and
a contrite heart, O God, thou wilt not despise.' ''

Not long after these words were written there
came the event that tried the faith of the strongest and drove them to their knees in voiceless,
agonising prayer. Under date of April 15, 1865,
this appears in the journal:

'' Every man's heart is broken to-day. The sorrow could not have been greater if in every hab-
itation in the land a loved one lay dead. One sees
no smiling faces to-day, and hears no more peals
of laughter on the streets. All is sad and solemn.

Thousands of flags had been flung to the breeze yesterday in honour of raising the national emblem over the ruins of Fort Sumter. Every window had its bright colours, and from every building the gay bunting streamed. But this morning, immediately after the news that Abraham Lincoln was dead, every banner was placed at half-mast, and draped in the symbols of mourning, while on every house front were festoons of somber black.''

Two weeks after the assassination of President Lincoln there was a delightful communion service at Pleasant Valley, near Harper's Ferry, when the saddened hearts of soldiers and delegates were gladdened as they drew close to the Lord. Remount Camp was to be broken up within a few days, and the men who had been companions through so many campaigns were to separate, so the service was arranged. Mr. Miller wrote of this primitive observance:

'' The appointments of the table were of a humble description. The plates were of tin, the cups pewter, the bread came from the commissary, the table cover was two religious newspapers, and over the bread were two small napkins, clean but not whole. Though the circumstances were so novel, and there was so much of discomfort, and the appointments of the table were so informal, yet the service was both interesting and profitable.''

Professor Stoever of Gettysburg College— whose house had been opened as a Christian Com-

mission hospital after the battle of Gettysburg—
was present, most unexpectedly, at the communion
in camp. Deeply impressed, he told of the day
in these words:

" The services were held in one of the chapels
erected by the Christian Commission, and conducted by two delegates, clergymen of evangelical
churches. The scene reminded one very much of
primitive apostolic times. Everyone present
seemed pervaded with the solemnity of the occasion. The chapel was filled with our veteran soldiers. As the men consecrated the elements contained in the humble vessels, it seemed as if all felt
that Jesus was present."

Soon after this communion service Mr. Miller
was called to Philadelphia and Baltimore, then
to Washington, where, to his own tasks for the
Army of the Shenandoah, he added the direction
of the Commission's work in the Army of the
Potomac and Sherman's Army. These heavy
duties were so well performed that in July it was
possible for him to resign his commission. The
resignation took effect on July 15.

During the last weeks of service he suffered
from fever, brought on by overwork. In July
he went to Atlantic City for a few days of
rest and change. The sea breeze proved to be the
tonic he needed. Within a few days he once more
felt strong and well.

The days at Atlantic City gave him leisure to

think back on the past and forward to the future. He spoke of his experience thus:

" It has been a good service to me, in that it has fitted me better for my life's great work. Some young men enter their professional life too early. Especially do those who enter the university do so before they are fitted for their work. . . . I came into the army just soon enough to prevent myself entering life at this same unfit age. Now I have seen a good deal of life . . . and I think I see a course that will fit me for more and greater usefulness. I have had opportunities of learning to read human nature, and perhaps know a little of the art of dealing with men. . . . I am satisfied with the dispensation that holds me back from early follies. . . .

" I can truly say that I have had such views of Christ's character, and have learned such love of Christ himself here, as I should not have gained for years anywhere else than in the army."

On July 12 Mr. Miller left Atlantic City for Washington. There he made out his final reports. Then he left for his home in Ohio, where he arrived—after making a number of visits on the way —on August 1.

At once he was besieged by requests to do work that would turn him aside from the ministry for an indefinite period. The American Union Commission, The American Railway Library Union, and the United Presbyterian Freedmen's Mission clamoured for his services. But he decided not to make his decision till he had taken time for study. In the meantime he prepared for his long-delayed licensure. He did not like to think of turning aside from the ministry, yet he trembled as he thought of the responsibility of standing in the pulpit:

"How shall I dare to open my lips or speak forth my words? A mistake here is a mistake fatal, eternally. As I think of these things my poor weak heart cries out, 'Oh, my God, who is sufficient for these things?' . . . I hear a voice that answers, 'My grace is sufficient for thee, and I will perfect strength in weakness.'"

The closing weeks of the summer were spent in the composition of sermons. For these the young student had received far better preparation in ministering to the needs of others than he could have received in the classroom alone.

THE THEOLOGICAL SEMINARY AND THE PASTORATE

We do not begin to understand what great waste we are allowing when we fail to put the true value on little opportunities of serving others. Somehow we get the feeling that any cross-bearing worth while must be a costly sacrifice, something that puts nails through our hands, something that hurts till we bleed. If we had an opportunity to do something heroic we say we could do it. But when it is only a chance to be kind to a neighbour, to sit up with him at night when he is sick, or to do something for a child, we never think for a moment that such little things are the Christ-like deeds God wants us to do, and so we pass them by and there is a great blank in our lives where holy service ought to be.—*From " In That Which Is Least," in " The Book of Comfort."*

We need great wisdom for the ministry of comfort. . . . We need to be sure that we understand God's way of giving comfort. . . . A professor in a theological seminary said to the students: " Never fail in any service to speak a word of comfort. No congregation, however small, ever assembles but there is in it at least one person in sorrow who will go away unhelped if in Scripture lesson, hymn, prayer, or sermon there is nothing to comfort a mourner or to lift up a heavy heart." An American preacher said, " I never look over a congregation of people waiting for a message from my life without thinking of what burdens many of them are carrying, through what struggles they are passing, what sorrows they are enduring, and how much they need comfort and encouragement that they may be able to go on in their pilgrimage journey."—*From " The Message of Comfort," in " A Heart Garden."*

CHAPTER V

THE THEOLOGICAL SEMINARY AND THE PASTORATE

(1865 to 1912)

Mr. Miller resumed his interrupted studies at the Allegheny Theological Seminary in the fall of 1865. His experiences during the war had so broadened his mind that he was able to make the most of his opportunities under Dr. John T. Pressley and Dr. David R. Kerr and their associates. The number then in the faculty was not nearly so large as in this and similar institutions to-day, but the men were all giants of intellectual and spiritual strength, and knew how to inspire the young men enrolled in their classes.

Fellow students who had valued Mr. Miller because of his unusual attainments marvelled at the way in which his character had been enriched by the service with the Christian Commission. They rejoiced in the opportunity for daily fellowship with one who was living so near to heaven that every word and act of his seemed to lift them close to God. His brotherliness of spirit, his earnestness of purpose, his humility and gentleness, and his never-flagging zeal won all who knew him.

His roommate in 1865—J. G. D. Findlay, later pastor at Newburgh, New York—said of him:

"I found him a genial and heartsome companion, and we passed the time pleasantly together. He was studious, fond of reading, and much interested in all Christian work. My association with him was especially helpful and uplifting."

Lifelong friendships were formed during these years. Perhaps the most intimate was with Charles A. Dickey, whom he assisted at a newly organised mission in Allegheny which grew into the Fourth United Presbyterian Church. There —in Sunday school, in prayer meeting, and the pulpit—he was a conscientious and unassuming associate. One of the great joys of later life in Philadelphia was friendship and fellowship with Dr. Dickey, then pastor of Bethany Church.

When the seminary celebrated its seventy-fifth anniversary, Dr. Miller wrote a hearty letter telling of his indebtedness to the institution. In this he said:

"By far the most lasting influences of my seminary life were its fellowships. . . . That which has stayed with me most persistently during these years has not been the theology, the church history, the New Testament Greek, or the Old Testament Hebrew, but the memory of certain men and the impressions which they made upon my life."

He completed his course in the spring of 1867. During the summer he accepted a call from the First United Presbyterian Church of New Wilmington, Pennsylvania, the seat of Westminster College, from which he had graduated five years earlier. His ordination and installation took place September 11, 1867, and he at once devoted himself heartily to the work of pulpit and pastorate. Being a college centre, the field gave inspiration for the most careful sermon preparation, and men who sat under his preaching in their student days—ministers, doctors, lawyers, and others—tell of the uplift which it brought to them. A number of men testified in later years that they were led by his strong personality and the spirit of his work to the determination to devote their lives to the gospel ministry.

Nor was it only the students who were helped by his preaching at New Wilmington. From the first there was a persuasiveness in tone and message, and an earnestness in utterance which made his preaching—to use the words of an admirer—" peculiarly his own." There was nothing stilted in his pulpit work, no straining after rhetorical or dramatic effect, but there was a simplicity, a directness, an elegance and richness in diction and illustration, combined with evident sincerity and earnestness that carried his messages directly to the heart.

It was evident to all who watched his work that he was winning a strong hold upon the hearts of children, because they always had a warm place in his heart's love. A mother still living in New Wilmington tells of the interest manifested in her only son by the young pastor, and of the affection which the child soon began to manifest in return. One of the ways in which he showed his interest in children and young people was in the encouragement he gave them to cultivate missionary gardens, or rows of corn or potatoes in their fathers' fields. Wherever there were children in the home there was a well-cared-for garden bed, or rows of corn or potatoes, or a tree in the orchard, the products of which were to be given to God. At Thanksgiving there would be a general ingathering of the fruits of the consecrated ground.

Though this first pastorate lasted but two years, nearly two hundred names were added to the church roll—eighty-five on confession of their faith and one hundred and thirteen by letter. Most men would have thought it unreasonable to expect such results in a circumscribed country field, but the young pastor discovered the people and went after them. He believed in calling repeatedly on all who would receive him. A physician, with whom he was then specially intimate, has since spoken of the list of more than one hundred families living within a radius of five miles from the village which his pastor visited during those two years of service.

He was not satisfied merely to receive members into the church; he felt that his duty was then

J. R. MILLER (1868)

just begun. The next thing was to train them for Christian service. This he was able to do with marked success. One who later became a pastor of some distinction gives this glimpse of methods that succeeded in his case:

" I had been for several years a member of the church, but I had never the courage to lead publicly in prayer. One Wednesday evening after prayer meeting he came to me personally and asked if I would not lead in prayer the next Wednesday evening. I was afraid, and would not consent. He talked with me very kindly and tenderly for a short time and asked me to think it over and pray about it. He said that he would pray also that the Lord would give me strength and courage to do as he asked. He said that I need not fear my being called on to pray until I could willingly give my consent. I was a green, backward country boy, and had it not been for his kind, sympathetic spirit and strong personal influence I could not have made the venture. But I did as he asked. The next steps were not easy, but his sympathy and suggestions helped me to continue after I had made the start."

Though his labours in this first pastorate were abundantly fruitful, Mr. Miller was not wholly satisfied with his ecclesiastical relationships. He held firmly to the great body of truth professed by the United Presbyterian Church, in which he had been reared, but he did not like the rule requiring the exclusive singing of the Psalms, and he felt that it was not honest for him to profess this as one of the articles of his Christian belief.

He had no prospect of a field of labour in any other denomination, and his people were daily becoming more devoted to him, when—in July, 1869—he wrote a long, tender letter to his father and mother, telling them of his scruples and of the decision he had formed, after much prayer and consideration, to resign his pastoral charge and to seek membership in the Presbyterian Church, U. S. A. He made no reflections whatever upon the Church in which he had been trained and by which he had been ordained. On the contrary, he acknowledged his deep indebtedness to the United Presbyterian Church, and to the godly parents who had so earnestly and faithfully taught him the way of life, and who had followed him with their earnest prayers all his days.

In August, 1869, he announced to the congregation his intention to resign the pastorate charge and asked them to join him in his request to presbytery for a dissolution of the relationship existing between them. The congregation reluctantly acquiesced in his request. By the action of the Presbytery of Mercer he was released August 24.

There was sorrow among the ministers and members of the United Presbyterian Church. There was a wide feeling among its ministers that the Lord had a work for Mr. Miller among them which would have been abundantly blessed. But those who knew the spirit of his life recognised the honesty and sincerity of heart with which he made the change, and followed him with their best wishes, their prayers and their unceasing interest. They recognised that the Lord had led him out into a wider field, and always rejoiced in the fact that his life had been so abundantly used.

While his relationship to the Church of his boyhood had ended, his interest in that Church was not at an end. Until the close of his life he was quick to acknowledge the great blessings that had come to him through the Church of his fathers. He recognised that although its membership and ministry were comparatively few in number, they were characterised by an intensity of life which made their witness and their service a blessing to the world. He recognised the strength and the sincerity of the convictions which governed its people and the tenacity with which these convictions were held. He made no effort to lead others to follow his example in transferring their membership from one church to the other. His answer to any who sought advice as to such a change was that they should be satisfied as to their own convictions of truth and duty, and then should faithfully follow them. To one who consulted him in reference to this matter, he said that not even the prospect of greater usefulness should lead one to make such a change, for God only knows where our lives can be most richly blessed; our place is to surrender our lives to God and seek to follow only where He leads.

After resigning his church at New Wilmington, Mr. Miller did not know what was to be his next step. No church had opened to him. But he felt he was following God's leading, so he was content to wait for further indications of God's will. He went to Allegheny, where he read and studied for two months.

Then came an invitation from the Bethany Presbyterian Church of Philadephia to undertake the pastorate. This was one of the very first calls issued after the reunion of the Old School and New School Churches, which was consummated in Pittsburgh, November 12, 1869. The invitation was accepted, and the new pastor began his new work November 21, 1869. On December 4 he was received by the Presbytery of Philadelphia.

On June 22, 1870, Mr. Miller was married to Miss Louise E. King of Argyle, New York, whom he had met in May, 1868, while attending the meeting of the General Assembly of the United Presbyterian Church in Argyle. From the day of his marriage Mrs. Miller was his inspiration and his helper in all his work. He was never weary of telling of his great debt to her. In his letters to young married people, he frequently told of what she was to him, and said that he could wish them no greater happiness than a home such as she was making for him. The secret of Mrs. Miller's helpfulness was not only her beautiful character, but her recognition of the fact that her husband belonged to those who listened to his preaching, who received him in their home, who read the publications he edited, or who were inspired by his books. That he might be free to serve them she saw to it that he was relieved of all home cares which she could take upon herself. In these efforts she was most successful.

At Bethany Mr. Miller gathered about him such an earnest and increasing band of workers that the church speedily outgrew the modest quarters in which he found it, and a larger building became necessary. In the problem incident to its construction, as in the spiritual problems of the field, he leaned heavily on a devoted session of which John Wanamaker was a member. The large Sunday school, of which Mr. Wanamaker was then —and is still—superintendent, called for much of the young pastor's time and thought. His relations with the young people were cordial and intimate, and he was able to persuade many of them to accept Christ.

When he became pastor at Bethany the membership was seventy-five. When he resigned in 1878 this was the largest Presbyterian church in Philadelphia, having about twelve hundred members.

The regard in which he was held there is indicated by the fact that fifteen years after he resigned the pastorate the session pleaded with him to return as one of the associate pastors of the church.

Nine years at Bethany so exhausted him that

he thought it wise to accept the call that came
to him from the new Broadway Presbyterian
Church of Rock Island, Illinois. He wished
greater opportunity for study than he could have
in the city parish. For nearly two years he remained in his new field, devoting himself without
reserve to the one hundred members who were
there to welcome him and the many who were received during his pastorate.

With great skill he adapted himself and his
methods to the peculiar conditions of his new
field. In order to make headway against dances,
tea parties and similar gatherings, which inter-
fered with church work, he organised a library
club. This met weekly in different homes. The
forty or fifty who attended the meetings were
helped and strengthened; many of them were led
to take a new interest in the church. He was also
a factor of moment in the life of the public-school
teachers, whom he encouraged in their work with
the young people by calling on them and entertain-
ing them in his home. The ministers of the town
—who had never worked together very well—were
given a vision of the possibilities of coöperation.

In 1880 Westminster College, his alma mater,
conferred on him the degree of Doctor of Divinity.
Later in the year came the invitation to undertake
editorial work for the Presbyterian Board of Publication which led him to Philadelphia. There
he became interested in the Hollond Mission,
a down-town work with a discouraging history.

He preached his first sermon in the little chapel of the mission January 2, 1881. A few days later he wrote this message to the people whose invitation to lead them he had accepted:

" You can help to make this chapel a warm, loving place, into which the weary, the sorrowing, the poor, the friendless, and the stranger will love to come. It costs but little to be kind, to reach out a cordial hand, to speak a few welcoming words; and yet whole families have been won by just such simple courtesies in church aisles. Do not wait for introductions. Those who enter our church doors are our guests, and we must make them feel at home.

" I desire to have a place in your confidence, and in your affections. The work of a true pastor is more, far more, than the faithful preaching of the Word. He is a physician of souls, and his work must be largely personal. I desire, therefore, to become the close, personal friend of everyone. I invite you to come to me freely for counsel and prayer in every matter that may concern your spiritual welfare. In sickness I want you to send for me. If you are in trouble, I claim the privilege of sharing it with you. I shall ever have a warm, ready sympathy, and a brother's helping hand for each of you when any burden presses, or any sorrow tries you. And in turn, I ask from you continual prayer, large patience, the firmest, truest friendship, a place in each home and heart, and ready coöperation in all the Master's work.''

The mission was organised as a church March 24, 1882. Dr. Miller was installed pastor April 23, 1882. At that time the church reported 259 members, while there were 1,024 in the Sunday school. During the sixteen months of the pastorate the church grew rapidly, both in numbers and influence.

On September 3, 1883, the pastoral relation was dissolved in order that Dr. Miller might devote himself to his editorial work. A month later Rev. William M. Paden became pastor. Dr. Miller assisted him in every way in his power, and the church grew rapidly.

In January, 1886, the hunger of the congregation for Dr. Miller's continued service led to the request that he become associated with Dr. Paden. His own hunger for the pastorate and intimate contact with the people led him to assume once more a burden that he had once decided was too great for him. For more than eleven years the new relation continued. Dr. Paden and Dr. Miller worked together in delightful harmony. For ten years Dr. Paden was a member of Dr. Miller's household.

In October, 1897, Dr. Paden accepted a call to Salt Lake City, Utah, and both pastors resigned. At this time the membership of the church was 1,164, and there were 1,475 members in the Sunday school. Dr. Miller acted as moderator of the session and supply of the church until June, 1898, when the new pastor was on the field. Then the church property was worth $125,000.

Concerning his resignation of the pastorate Dr. Miller wrote to a friend:

"In one sense it is a pleasure to me to lay this burden down. My duty has seemed very clear in the matter. My editorial and literary work have been growing continually during recent years, and now fill my hands so full that I cannot in justice to myself undertake any extended work outside."

But the busy man could not be satisfied out of the pulpit. Every Sunday he was busy in some church, after a week whose evenings were spent calling on those who needed his help. To a Philadelphia pastor he wrote of his desire to keep his Sundays occupied:

"You know I am now free from Sunday work and I need not say to you that at any time when I can relieve you either for one service or for a whole Sunday when you want to rest a little, it will not only be a privilege but a real pleasure to me to do it. I would not accept compensation for any such service."

A few weeks after concluding his work at Hollond Dr. Miller moved with his family to Germantown, one of the delightful residence sections of Philadelphia. He had made up his mind not to accept an active pastorate. He thought he might learn of some little church that needed him where he might preach once a Sunday, conduct a Bible class, and do pastoral work.

The appearance of the desired work was announced in a letter to one who inquired about his future movements:

"There is a piece of summer work in West Philadelphia which is pressing very much upon my heart at present and which I may decide to take up."

In the summer he assisted in the tent where this work was being carried on. In the fall a small frame chapel was bought. This was dedicated October 29, 1898, and the services were continued there. On October 29, 1899, St. Paul Church was organised with sixty-six members. Dr. Miller who had given much help and encouragement during the intervening months was chosen temporary supply.

The church prospered. It was located in a rapidly growing section of the city, and it had a pastor who was speedily on the ground when a new family moved in whose members were not connected with some other church. On May 11, 1900, a lot was purchased, and in this a stone chapel was erected at a cost of about $20,000. This was dedicated March 24, 1901. Thus—in less than three years—a discouraged group of workers, inspired by Dr. Miller, had become an active church, possessed of a property worth $35,000.

During these early years Dr. Miller would not accept a salary. Later, when it seemed wise to permit the church to provide a salary, he managed in one way or other to restore every dollar to the church. During the fourteen years of his connection with St. Paul he did not profit financially by his service. He felt that he should live on his salary as editor, and that the salary provided by the church should always be used in the varied activities of the congregation.

Additions were made to the church building until—on October 7, 1906—the beautiful $150,000 property was dedicated. One month later Dr. Miller—who had continued as stated supply all these years—was called as pastor. The installation followed on December 12.

The relationship thus established continued till January 1, 1912, when Dr. Miller was made Pastor Emeritus. Rev. J. Beveridge Lee, D.D., who had been associated with him in the work for two years, then became the pastor of a church of 1,397 members and a Sunday school of 1,193 members.

Thus, during thirty-nine years, Dr. Miller served three Philadephia churches. He had taken charge of three struggling fields, which he left among the largest churches in the city.

The annual growth of these churches was marvellous. During the nine years he was connected with the Bethany Church, 1870-78, 1,620 persons were received into the membership of that church, making an average of 180 a year; during the sixteen years of his association with the Hollond Memorial Church, 1881-1897, 1,817 persons were received, an average of 113 each year; and during the fourteen years of his connection with St. Paul Church, 1898-1912, 1,904 persons were received, an average of 136 a year. In the thirty-nine years of his pastoral relations with these three churches, 5,341 persons were received, making an average of 137 for every year. The largest number of accessions was in Bethany, in 1876, when 367 were received on confession, and 68 by letter, making a total of 435. Hollond received 175 members in 1894, and St. Paul 251 in 1909.

THE PASTOR AT WORK

No name of Christ means more to us in the interpretation of His life and love than Friend. We are not only to tell those we teach of the beauty of the friendship of Christ, we must interpret that friendship in ourselves. What Christ was to those to whom He became a personal friend we must be to those we make our friends. He did not seem to do many things for them. He did not greatly change their condition. He did not make life easier for them. It was in a different way that His friendship helped them. He gave them sympathy. They knew He cared for them, and then the hard things meant less to them. It is a great thing for a boy to know that a good man is his friend, is interested in him. To many a lad it is the beginning of a new life for him. "If you will be my friend I can be a man," said a pupil in a mission school to his teacher who had spoken to him the first really kind word he ever had heard. The greatest moment in anyone's life is when he first realises that Christ is his Friend.—*From " The Master and the Children," in " The Book of Comfort."*

Our errand in this world is in a small way the same that Christ's errand was. He does not now . . . go about doing good—we are to go for Him. The only hands Christ has for doing kindness are our hands. The only feet He has to run the errands of love are our feet. The only voice He has to speak cheer . . . is our voice.—*From " The Lesson of Love."*

CHAPTER VI

THE PASTOR AT WORK

IN 1910 a younger minister in the West wrote to Dr. Miller asking him to tell him how to make his ministry a success. The letter sent in reply concluded with these paragraphs:

"Cultivate love for Christ and then live for your work. It goes without saying that the supreme motive in every minister's life should be the love of Christ. 'The love of Christ strengtheneth me,' was the keynote of St. Paul's marvellous ministry. But this is not all. If a man is swayed by the love of Christ he must also have in his heart love for his fellow men. If I were to give you what I believe is one of the secrets of my own life, it is, that I have always loved people. I have had an intense desire all of my life to help people in every way; not merely to help them into the church, but to help them in their personal experiences, in their struggles and temptations, their quest for the best things in character. I have loved other people with an absorbing devotion. I have always felt that I should go anywhere, do any personal service, and help any individual, even the lowliest and the highest. The Master taught me this in the washing of His disciples' feet, which showed His heart in being willing to do anything to serve His friends. If you want to have success as a winner of men, as a helper of people, as a pastor of little children, as the friend of the tempted and imperilled, you must love them and have a sincere desire to do them good.

" Right here is where professionalism works so much of its mischief. I have heard men say that they would not see people, say, at certain hours of the day, because these were hours they had set apart for something else in a professional way. I have heard of ministers refusing to go out on stormy nights because they thought they had done their work for that day. This kind of spirit will never succeed in the highest way. It may bring a man up to a noted professional standing but it will never make him a real helper of his fellow men. The man that wants you is the man that you want to see. When you love men you must love every man and any man. I mean whoever needs you you must seek to help, whatever the cost may be, in whatever little way you may be able to serve him.

" It seems that your secret of success just now will be, not in developing the professional ideals, not in following any rules which you have learned in the seminary, but in caring for people with such intensity that you will be ready to make any self-sacrifice to do them good.

" If you would win men for Christ you must win them first to yourself. That is, you must make them believe in you, love you. Mary and her lamb have a lesson for us. ' " What makes the lamb love Mary so? " the eager children cry. " Oh, Mary loves the lamb, you know," the teacher did reply.' If you love people they will love you and you can lead them anywhere and make anything of them it is possible to make."

This letter was valuable because its writer had lived out every statement in it. He loved his people. He forgot himself. He delighted to quote the words of Alexander Maclaren, "To efface self is one of a preacher's first duties." His people loved him because he thought nothing of himself and everything of them.

His self-effacement was never more apparent than when he was in the pulpit. He seemed to be unconscious of the existence of J. R. Miller. He seemed to think only of God, and the people; of his Friend and those whom he longed to introduce to his Friend. And he had his reward. Thousands learned from his life the way to God.

A correspondent of *The British Monthly* once wrote of his sermons:

" Though void of the sensational, they are never commonplace. He never loses sight of the fact that they are to supply spiritual food and instruction to immortal souls, and right royally do they perform their mission. All are marked by simplicity of speech, lofty ideals, tender appeals, the statement of the heart's great need, and the magnifying of the all-powerful Helper. In them there is neither theorising nor temporising; no man can mistake their meaning—all is plain, direct, earnest, forceful. Men listen attentively, reverently, prayerfully; they instinctively feel that the preacher is expressing great truths, that he is setting forth their spiritual needs, that he is translating into words the nobler longings of their lives. ' Thou art the man ' is what every thoughtful person thinks of himself when listening to Dr. Miller's earnest condemnation of sin and to his pleadings for more of purity, usefulness and holiness. It is little wonder then that people who sit under his preaching strive to lead clean, helpful lives, and to do the will of the Master."

He never forgot the universal need of comfort. "We forget how much sorrow there is in the world," he one day remarked. "Why, there are hearts breaking all about us. I have made it a rule of my ministry never to preach a sermon without giving some word of comfort to the sorrowing. In every congregation there is sure to be some soul hungering for consolation."

The mails brought him many such letters as this:

"Will you let me write you a word of gratitude and appreciation? I wish that I might tell you how much you are to others, but the lines you quoted in your sermon of November 27 best express my thought.

"Through the reading of Darwin's writings, and other things in my life, I was left with faith in nothing except a vague, uncertain belief in God and immortality which was half obscured by doubt. But through the force and beauty of your life and words my thoughts have broadened and faith in God and the Christ Child, and the possibility of true and beautiful lives have come back to me. Though the questionings remain unanswered I am content to forget them in the desire for an unselfish and sincere life."

Another listener who was helped wrote:

" Where do you get all your good sermons?
Straight from God! You make them such a part
of one's life I know it must be possible to live
them even if I do fail. Even trying makes one
better and happier.

" This little note only wants to thank you for
your preaching and for your influence which has
done and is doing a good work in me."

All parts of a service conducted by Dr. Miller
were made helpful and inspiring. His prayers
especially were strengthening and uplifting.
They took one into the presence of God, whom he
seemed to see as he was speaking. In 1904 a
famous minister who preached for him wrote,
after returning home:

" In the morning I found it very hard work
to ask God's blessing on such a sermon as seemed
to be inevitable. I would gladly have remained
at home, but this was childish. Your prayer broke
my heart, and I had a few minutes of humble confession and supplication as they were singing,
which were refreshing to my soul. I would travel
the distance between my home and your church
to hear you pray."

It was a delight to Dr. Miller's people to know
that this prince in prayer was interceding for
them. They understood that he had his special
prayer list, on which were the names of all who
sought prayers for any reason, as well as those
who, Dr. Miller felt, should be remembered. In

addition to this, he had his regular list, on which the names of every member of the church and congregation appeared. The year was begun with a month of prayer for these. The fact was announced by a note like this, put in the hands of all members in December:

" January is to be our month of prayer. Every member of the church and all others who desire to be included will be remembered personally, by name, on a particular day. All whose names begin with A will be remembered January 1, all beginning with B will be remembered January 2, all beginning with C January 3, and so on.

" As your name begins with A, you will be remembered next Monday. This notice is sent to you that you may write to Dr. Miller before your day, mentioning any special requests for prayer you may have, either for yourself or for any of your friends. These letters will all be confidential."

Another letter mailed to the people was the annual pastoral greeting sent in September, after the summer vacation was over and workers were returning to their places. These letters never were perfunctory—they seemed a part of Dr. Miller's self. Here are paragraphs from one:

" Our past is full of splendid inspiration. The way God has helped us has been marvellous. We have increased greatly in numbers. But better far than that, blessing has gone out from this church and has helped many lives.

" More than ever before, our church must be

this year a church of Christ. It must be a house of bread. When the hungry come here, they must be fed. When the sorrowing come, they must be comforted. When the lonely come, they must find love and companionship.

"Everyone has a share all his own, in the responsibility, something to do which no other one can do to make the church what it ought to be this year. Every boy and every girl has a bit of work to do. What can we do? We may invite people to come with us. We may welcome those who come, and make them feel at home. We may be always here ourselves. Our place is here. Let us not scatter our work, but put all our strength and influence in right here. This is the best way we can help our Master. We may make every service here a little better by always being present.

"There is something else: We may love one another. That is our church creed. There is no place in the religion of our Master for selfishness, grumpiness, touchiness, bad temper, bitter feeling, disobligingness, ' Little children, love one another.'

"We want to make the church this year the homiest church in our city. This is our church home. Let us always meet as members of the same family—cordially, cheerfully, affectionately. In our own homes we are hospitable to everyone who comes to our doors. Let us show hospitality also to all strangers who come to our church. The Bible says, ' Forget not to show love unto strangers: for thereby some have entertained angels unawares.' Let us watch for angels.

"I am deeply conscious of the need of divine help as we pledge ourselves to each other and to our Master for another year. We can do nothing ourselves alone. But the divine help is ready if we will do our part. When Christ sent out his disciples, saying, ' As the Father hath sent me, even so send I you,' he also breathed on them, and said, ' Receive ye the Holy Spirit.' The Master is ready to send us out, and also to breathe his Spirit into our hearts to prepare us for holy life and blessed service. Shall we receive the Spirit? ''

The mails always played an important part in Dr. Miller's pastoral work. The printed letters were merely an incident; his daily habit was the writing of a number—sometimes scores—of letters to members who needed them. To discouraged workers the postman would deliver a letter of cheer. Young Christians would be given an opportunity to read a message of counsel or suggestion. Those struggling with temptation would be apt to find that the pastor had in some mysterious way become possessed of their secret and had written to them in their need. All sick members of the church would receive a letter on the afternoon of Saturday before communion. Those about to unite with the church were sure of a letter. No exception was made to this rule even when he was on his vacation in Europe. Learning through an officer of the church the names of those who were to confess Christ at the communion during his absence, he wrote an encouraging letter to each one, and gave instructions that a helpful booklet should be sent to each as a memorial of the service. After the communion another letter was always mailed to those whose names he had placed on the roll of the church. Here is one of the after-communion letters:

"No words can tell my pleasure at the privilege which I have of receiving you into the church. I know how earnest and sincere your life has been. It gives me, therefore, the greatest pleasure to be permitted to take you by the hand and welcome you into the communion of the church and the fellowship of Christian people. I know well that while you have been happy in your religious experience, you will find new blessing and new joy in taking this public step. It is always so—however earnest one may have been as a Christian and however sincere, there is something in the public confession of Christ which always brings a blessing with it. You will therefore have great joy and deep peace and I am sure your influence and usefulness will be largely extended. May God bless you and your dear wife and your children all."

To another young Christian he said:

"One of the mottoes which I give my young people continually is, 'Always keep sweet whatever the experiences may be.' Let me give this to you as the aim of your life. Always keep sweet. You have fallen into the habit of being blue sometimes. This is not a beautiful thing in life, and I am sure it only makes you unhappy and makes others unhappy. A little word of our Saviour's says, 'In the world ye shall have tribulations,' but he adds, 'In me ye shall have peace; therefore be of good cheer.' You want to learn to trust Christ with all the affairs of your life, to let him keep you and care for you and provide for you, and shape your circumstances. If you do this, every day committing your life to God, trusting him, and then going forward in sweet confidence and joy, you may be sure of peace all the while.

" I think I have given you enough for one lesson. Please write me soon and tell me how you get on. I want to hear from you often, especially until you get well started in this new life. You have turned to me as your friend and I want to help you."

Many of the young converts were encouraged to be present at the prayer meeting, and to take part, and so many responded that the weekly meetings were always a joy and inspiration. Dr. Miller would speak only about ten minutes; the remainder of the hour was filled by many eager participants. No wonder the meeting became famous throughout the city, and beyond. Once members of the senior class in Princeton Theological Seminary visited many prayer meetings in New York and Philadelphia, and then decided which was the most helpful. In the ballot Dr. Miller's prayer meeting led all the rest.

Dr. Miller was as faithful on Sunday as on week nights. He was not content to attend preaching service only; he was a regular attendant at the Sunday school, where he taught a large and enthusiastic class of women. At Hollond the membership of his class was about four hundred; his class at St. Paul was half as large. His loyalty to the Sunday school was delightfully indicated by a little girl whose parents asked her if

J. R. MILLER (1875)

she knew Dr. Miller. " Oh, yes! " was the reply, " he goes to our Sunday school! "

In the Christian Endeavour Society, too, this young people's pastor who never grew old was a constant encourager and helper. He never forgot a meeting. When in Europe in 1896 he sent this message for the monthly consecration meeting of his society:

" No matter where we go—away from home, away from work—we can never get away from God. We must be careful to live so that we shall never want to get away from ourself; and we must also live so that we shall never desire to get away from God."

He was just as acceptable and effective in his work with the older members. He knew how to take them, and he could get along with them when no one else could. One of his elders once said:

" I do not recall ever having seen any indication of a factional difference or lack of harmony in the church during Dr. Miller's pastorate. He had a way of anticipating trouble. If he saw any person or any organisation which showed indications of getting out of touch with the work, it was his custom to go to the one or the group, as the case might be, give them a few encouraging words, tell them how much he depended upon them, and tell them how much they had helped him in his work, and show them ways of further assistance and service. His matchless tact, as well as his example, kept everyone in harmony."

In every church to which he ministered he inspired young men to give themselves to the work of the ministry. Two of the members of one of his Christian Endeavour Societies who took this step afterwards wrote to him telling of his part in their lives. One said:

" I have never forgotten the care you gave to me and the inspiration I received from you as pastor and friend during college and seminary years."

The other wrote from the foreign mission field:

" I can never, never repay the debt I owe to you. And as it was with me so it was with countless others. I thank God fervently for what your life has meant to me."

Love for the young people led Dr. Miller to consent to direct the Wellesley school for young women, which was financed by John Wanamaker. Dr. Miller looked on this as part of his pastoral work. For several years he gave much time and thought to the young women and their teachers, and both teachers and pupils gratefully acknowledged their indebtedness to him. One of the teachers in the school he had first met when pastor at Rock Island, Illinois. There he encouraged her with the words: " Move right on, with a brave, cheerful heart. The Master is with you and your work cannot fail." Through him she was invited to Philadelphia and there he continued to say the words that enabled her to go on to noble achievements.

But the heart of Dr. Miller's pastoral work was not the school, or his association with the young people, or his helpful letters. The greatest thing in his life among the churches was his habit of calling from house to house.

Once a visitor to St. Paul Church looked from the characteristic Sunday evening audience that filled the building, to the speaker who could be heard only with difficulty in the back of the room, and said: "How does he do it? Where is that man's power?" One standing near said: "Oh, sir! if you were in trouble, and Dr. Miller called on you or wrote to you, you would never ask that question again. He has built up this church by his wonderful pastoral work."

His pastoral work did not mean simply making a specified number of rounds each year among his members. He had only three or four evenings a week for calls—the other evenings he was at the church; but in these evening hours he made more calls than any other pastor in Philadelphia. He had a way of learning just when and where he was needed.

Wherever he went he inspired to earnest living. Thousands would join in the message of one who was privileged to receive his calls, "The sweetness of his presence in our home was just like what I think the presence of Jesus must have been in the home of Mary and Martha." One on

whom he called frequently said he lived in accordance with the simple words of what he called
his creed, " Jesus and I are friends."

The way he was welcomed in the home of suffering is well shown by a letter from a physician:

" The comfort you ministered to our dear Mabel
in her dying hours has ever been held by us as
too sacred for discussion. I have often heard that
pleading voice as she anxiously turned her eyes
to you and said, ' Don't go, Dr. Miller.' "

The calls were made on rich and poor alike, but
he felt that he was needed more in the homes of
the poor, and he was there more frequently.

Another principle that guided him as he made
his calls he once stated thus:

" If there is a house which nobody wants to
visit, or a person in that house whom everyone
avoids, I feel that I should be derelict in my duty
as a Christian minister, and recreant to the Master, whose I am, and whom I serve, if I did not go
to that house and try to comfort, help and save
that person."

To one who found fault with him because he
seemed to pay attention to one girl in the congregation more than to a companion, he made an
explanation that was in perfect accord with the
declaration just quoted. He said:

" You speak of Mary and Alice. You think that
I have been drawn more to the former than to the

latter. This is scarcely the case. Mary may have appealed to me more just because she needs more help. Alice is comfortable and happy, surrounded by love and kindness and does not need so much as Mary does. Somehow my heart goes out first of all, and most deeply, toward those who need most. For many years I have sought to be helpful to those whom other persons are not likely to help. People who are happy and comfortable, with many friends about them, do not therefore appeal to me in the same way as those who lack these earthly blessings. I think Alice has a beautiful character. I want to know her better. I want to be her close, personal friend. I am sure I shall get to love her very deeply and truly. But I have not felt that God has called me to help her in any special way. Perhaps she may need me more than I imagine. I should love to be helpful to her in any way I can be.

"I think this statement will show you just how the matter rests in my mind. It is not so much a comparison of the two girls as to their worth, their beauty of character, their nobleness of womanhood, but rather a comparison of the appeals they make respectively to me. Do I make my meaning clear?"

All who knew him marvelled as they saw how full his days were of varied service. Frequently some one would tell him he was doing the work of three men. He would insist that this was not true. Once he said:

"It is only one man's work. Most ministers have their 'free Mondays' and their evenings for symphony concerts, and all that sort of thing, or sitting down at home. I give up every hour to activity of some sort. I am very busy at the office all day; my people are there with their troubles all the time. In the evening I go out visiting sick people and others. At about 9:30 I return and have an hour with my family before they scatter off. And I think my evenings save me from growing old. I feel younger every year.''

But at last the burden proved too heavy, and the pastor resigned his last charge. In telling the church session of his purpose, he said:

'' It has been a dream of mine that I might continue in the work, in the co-pastorate which has brought to me such joy and such delightful fellowship, ending my days at St. Paul's. None but myself can ever know how dear the people are to me. They have been gathered one by one with thought and love. In many homes I have been in times of suffering or sorrow and with hundreds I have walked in experiences of joy or of pain which have bound them to me in very sacred ties. The church has come to be to me, in a very real sense, like my own family, and I have thought that it would be a joy to spend my last days among the people and be buried among them.

'' But the condition of my health in recent months is such that I cannot hope to carry any important part of the work hereafter. It seems wise, therefore, that I should resign my position at an early day.''

When the congregation met to act on his resignation a letter was read, in which he said:

" We have had a good time together as pastor and people these dozen years. Last Sunday as I looked into the faces of the great congregation sitting at the Lord's table, I could not help recalling the first communion in the wooden chapel, twelve years ago. The little handful has become a great throng, and instead of the rude little building where we broke bread that morning we sat last Sunday in our beautiful church edifice. A wonderful story lies between these two communions—a story of love, of Christian fellowship, of self-denial and service, of earnest Christian work, of prayer, of sacrificial life, of joy and sorrow, of great spiritual blessing.

" I want to say to you, friends, that St. Paul's is the crowning joy of my life. It has been a most sacred privilege to live with you, to grow up with you in this church, to be your friend, to share your burdens, to help you through hard places. While I may no longer be your pastor, no dissolution of an ecclesiastical relation will break the personal bond that binds you to me in love. I hope to live among you as one of you while God lets me stay in this world. When I can be of any comfort or help to any of you, it will be a joy to me."

His last official message was sent to the elders of the church at Christmas, 1911. He closed with these words:

" May the Christmas Day mean more to you than any Christmas before has meant. May it be the real coming anew of Christ into your heart, not as a mere sentiment, but as a living power, transforming you more and more into the divine beauty, and imparting to you divine strength, which shall make your life henceforth a richer influence, a greater power than ever it has been before. You have a large responsibility in your position; you will meet it with faith and courage."

THIRTY-TWO YEARS AN EDITOR

Loyalty to Christ is shown in using our life in whatever way we may be able and may have opportunity to use it. You cannot be loyal to Christ and not be good. You cannot be loyal to Christ and not be always abounding in His work.—*From "Loyalty to Christ," in "The Wider Life."*

If we fail to make little garden spots round about us where we live and where we work, we are not fulfilling our mission, nor obeying the teaching that we should be in the world what He was in the world, repeating His life of love among men.— *From "Upper Currents."*

Whatever else we may do or may not do, we should certainly train ourselves to be kind. It may not be an easy lesson to learn, for its secret is forgetting ourselves and thinking of others—and this is always hard. But it can be learned. To begin with, there must be a gentle heart to inspire the gentle life. We must love people—if we do not, no training, no following of rules, will ever make us kind. But if the heart be full of the love of Christ, the disposition will be loving, and it will need no rules to teach the lips ever gracious words and the hands to do always the things of kindness, and to do them always at the right time. Too many wait till it is too late to be kind.—*From "The Ministry of Kindness," in "Upper Currents."*

CHAPTER VII

THIRTY-TWO YEARS AN EDITOR

DURING the closing months of his service with the Christian Commission Dr. Miller thought seriously of turning aside from the ordained ministry that he might devote himself to a wider ministry by the pen. Already he felt the longing to give to the world burning messages that would reach hundreds of thousands instead of the few hundreds who might be attracted by his preaching. To some of his intimate friends he outlined a plan of preparation for newspaper work to which he had all but committed himself. He thought of taking a year for study in Edinburgh, to be followed by a year in Germany. As he travelled he proposed to live in the homes of the people that he might learn of their life and their problems, and so be able to carry back to America an enlarged knowledge of the human heart and its needs. This he felt would be necessary if he was to be successful in the best sense in the work of which he dreamed. Letters were written to the editors of several metropolitan newspapers telling of his plans, and asking for an engagement to write articles about his experiences; in this way he would be able to pay a portion of the expense of the projected two years abroad.

Yet he could not give up the ministry for which he had been preparing when the war interrupted his course. Thoughts of foreign travel and of later editorial work were put aside, while he returned to the seminary and entered the pastorate.

But God was planning for him the joy of combining the pastorate and editorial work. During the remainder of his seminary days and while he was at New Wilmington, Bethany Church, Philadelphia, and Rock Island, articles from his pen were welcomed by the religious papers. When —in 1875—Henry C. McCook, D.D., of Philadelphia, discontinued his weekly articles on the International Sunday School Lessons for *The Presbyterian*, published in Philadelphia, he recommended Dr. Miller as his successor. The lessons of the new writer were prepared in such a helpful manner that when the Presbyterian Board of Publication began to look for an assistant to work with John W. Dulles, D.D., the Editorial Secretary, Dr. McCook suggested the young pastor at Rock Island. Dr. McCook had planned the early periodical publications of the Board, had suggested their name—'' The Westminster Lesson Helps ''—and had been for a time their editor. So the recommendation was favourably considered, and on March 15, 1880, Dr. Dulles wrote to Dr. Miller asking him if he would consider becoming assistant to the Editorial Secretary. He said frankly that the position would not be conspicuous, but assured him that there would be opportunity for abundant service.

The call to service always meant more to Dr. Miller than conspicuous place, so he did not hesitate to reply favourably. On March 23 Dr. Dulles wrote a second letter, defining the position more clearly, and stating his feeling that while an old editor may be as hard for an assistant to get along with as an old pastor, he felt there could be no room for friction, since both editor and assistant had one aim only—not self, but results for the kingdom of Christ.

His belief in Dr. Miller was justified. The two worked together in harmony and affection so long as Dr. Dulles had strength for his duties. The experiment was so successful that Dr. McCook later wrote:

" I am sure that there is nothing which I have done, directly or indirectly, or nothing which I have influenced to be done, which I regard as so well done as the recommendation of you for the position you now hold."

As soon as it was known that Dr. Miller planned to remove to Philadelphia, overtures were made to him by one of the churches of the city which desired him to become pastor in connection with his new work. Dr. Miller looked with favour on the proposition, but Dr. Dulles, writing in behalf of the Board, urged that it would be impossible to do justice to the Board and that church at the same time. This was a perfectly natural suggestion, for Dr. Miller's remarkable ability to do the work of three men had not yet been proved. The history of the next thirty years was to show that he was not to be judged by the standards set for the average man.

When Dr. Miller entered on his work the Board's only periodicals were *The Westminster Teacher, The Westminster Lesson Leaf,* the *Senior Quarterly, The Sabbath School Visitor, The Sunbeam* and *The Presbyterian Monthly Record.* While he had something to do with all of these it was *The Westminster Teacher* that benefited most by his painstaking, sympathetic writing. The lesson pages were enriched by his extremely practical and spiritual comments on the lessons. His articles were soon eagerly awaited by pastors, superintendents and teachers all over the country. Soon workers in Great Britain asked for the *Teacher,* attracted most of all by his writing.

In 1890, in writing to a reader who thanked him for these lesson articles, he said:

" My only aim has been to make the Bible teaching plain and simple for ordinary Sunday-school teachers, especially to suggest to them the practical applications which they may make in teaching. I have always felt myself, in reading commentaries and lesson helps, the lack of this practical character. That is, while men have made the meaning of the text clear enough, they have not given suggestions which will aid teachers in applying the words of inspiration to the common life of those they teach. Most Sunday-school teachers lack the skill themselves to draw inferences and suggest applications, and therefore need, I think, such simple helps as I have tried in these years to give them.''

On January 1, 1881, the magazine was enlarged that Dr. Miller might have more pages for his work, and that provision might be made for some of the features for which his brilliant editorial mind was arranging. This was the beginning of development that continued to the end of Dr. Miller's editorial service. Year after year the magazine was improved; always it kept pace with the practical visions of Sunday-school leaders, among whom Dr. Miller was numbered from the beginning. But through all the changes of more than twenty-five years his explanatory notes and lesson comments were continued, because subscribers insisted on having them. In later years the attempt was made several times to omit them, but clamour was so great that they had to be restored. This was a surprise to the author; in his modesty he thought that people would be growing weary of his work, and would wish to be led in their study by some more up-to-date man. But it was the verdict of all who knew him—whether personally or through his writing—that he was always up-to-date; his daily heart-contact with people in their

homes and in his office taught him the secret of
perpetual youth and almost universal acceptance.

The Westminster Teacher was always very dear
to him. Only a little while before his death, when
the slightest exertion was wearisome, he asked an
associate to spend an hour with him in his home,
in order that he might talk over plans for the
magazine for the year 1913.

Dr. Dulles coöperated with his assistant as he
outlined the needs of the Sunday school for addi-
tional periodicals. When their plans were laid
before the Board of Publication, they were usually
adopted with alacrity. At the beginning of 1881
the first copies of the *Junior Lesson Leaf* and the
German Lesson Leaf were issued. *Forward* made
its appearance in 1882. *The Morning Star* followed in 1883. Two years later the *Junior Quarterly* was launched.

From 1885 to 1894 earnest thought and untiring
labour were devoted to the development of the
periodicals already on the list, and to remarkably
discriminating book work. Dr. Miller—who became Editorial Superintendent in 1887—was a
genius in securing and encouraging authors whom
he wished to have in the catalogue of the Board.

In 1894 began another period of expansion. In
four years the *Lesson Card,* the *Intermediate
Quarterly,* the *Question Leaf* and the *Blackboard*
were introduced to the Sunday schools. In 1899
the *Home Department Quarterly* followed. Then
came the *Primary Quarterly* in 1901, the *Normal*

Quarterly and the *Bible Roll* in 1902, the *Beginners Lessons*—forerunner of the *Graded Lessons* —in 1903, the *Primary Teacher* in 1906, the *Graded Lessons* for Beginners, Primary, Junior, Intermediate and Senior departments, in 1909-1912, and *The Westminster Adult Bible Class* in 1909. *The Sabbath School Visitor*—the Board's oldest periodical—became *The Comrade* in 1909.

In the meantime *The Presbyterian Monthly Record* became *The Church at Home and Abroad,* and was transferred to other hands by direction of the General Assembly. The *Junior Lessons,* the *German Lesson Leaf,* the *Question Leaf* and the *Blackboard* were discontinued, as their place was taken by other publications.

The total issue of the periodicals on the list was, in 1911, 66,248,215 copies. In 1880, when Dr. Miller became assistant editor, the total was 9,256,386.

Editors and publishers of other Sunday-school periodicals generally agreed that each new periodical of the Westminster series set a new standard, which they were glad to keep before them as they made their plans. Both in editorial excellence and mechanical appearance the periodicals and magazines have always been models.

The secret of this continued success was that Dr. Miller was never satisfied. He was glad to hear from readers who complimented him on producing what—as they enthusiastically said— " could not be made better." But it was always his desire to make every publication of a new year superior to that issued during the old year. " Now what can we do to make the publication better next year? " was a question that became familiar to members of the editorial staff. Then he helped them plan the improvement—helped them so skillfully that they thought they had done the planning. He let them think so, for it meant more to him that the work was done than that the praise should be given to him. He was always glad to pass on the praise to others.

He was a master in developing and inspiring assistants who could help him with the varied work of the office. His staff was so well organised that it continued to do efficient work if he was away from the office for a few days or a few weeks. Yet he always knew all about every periodical. All correspondence came to his desk, and was answered by him; all arrangements with writers were made by him; for years he read the manuscripts submitted; all proof came to him, and was carefully scanned, sometimes read word by word. In short, every slightest detail of office management was understood by him. Even the coming of associates chosen by the Board for his relief was not the signal for losing touch with any part of the work. He had the rare ability to know all that was going on while giving associates full opportunity for development.

To every one of the periodicals Dr. Miller gave his best thought. Yet there were three of the

publications which were especially dear to him—
The Westminster Teacher, as already noted; the
Home Department Quarterly; and *Forward.*

It was his idea that the members of the Home
Department should be given a magazine prepared
for them especially. He was not pleased with
the suggestion made by some houses that—for the
sake of economy—this publication should be in
large part a reprint of the *Senior Quarterly.* His
knowledge of the homes of the people, especially
the homes of invalids and busy mothers who make
up a large proportion of Home Department membership, made him anxious to give them an interpretation of the lesson adapted to their peculiar
needs. It was his plan to follow the verse-by-
verse comment on the text with a message for each
day on some truth in the lesson. This was done
with such marvellous skill that many a reader
would feel that the paragraphs were special individual messages, and that the editor somehow
must have learned of his circumstances and his
needs. This impression was intensified by an introductory letter in each number addressed " To
the Home Department Students." In one of these
he said:

" There probably are a great many shut-ins
among Home Department pupils—persons who
cannot get away from their homes, some who
cannot leave their rooms or even their beds. You
must not feel that because you are shut in, unable
to go out into the big world, therefore you need

to be especially lonely or that you cannot take your part in the work of Christ. Some of the most active and efficient Christian workers I know are Christians who cannot go out at all, month after month.''

Another quarter he said:

'' This *Quarterly* is used chiefly in homes. Nothing in this world is worthy of more thought, prayer and effort than the home. Sometimes mothers of young children think that their life is one of privation, because they are shut in so closely and miss many of the bright and happy things that so many people enjoy. But the mother's work is so sacred, and means so much to her children, that she can well afford to miss a good many things outside which would be very pleasant.''

Often such an invitation as this was given:

'' I shall always be glad to have letters from the Home Department students, bringing to me, when they so desire, questions, difficulties, experiences of trouble or sorrow, in which I may be permitted to give a little assistance.''

The letters came in numbers. And always a warm personal message was sent in answer that brought correspondents nearer to the editor's Friend.

Dr. Miller always emphasised as a prime requisite for successful editorial work that a writer must prepare his work with individuals in mind. To an associate to whom he committed the *Home*

Department Quarterly he expressed his feeling thus:

" Try writing each paragraph with some definite home in mind. Think of yourself as a pastor giving help and counsel to the invalids or the burdened in that home. Then your work will have the lifelike quality, and you will hear from many who will wonder how you came to know of them."

It was owing to just such writing as this that Dr. Miller saw the circulation of the *Home Department Quarterly* grow within twelve years from nothing to 128,000.

The story of the development of *Forward,* the Sunday-school paper for young people, is one of the most striking evidences of Dr. Miller's editorial sagacity and ability. When he began his work for the Board he dreamed of a paper that would give the young people in the Sunday school the best stories and general articles, and a page of wholesome, cheerful Christian counsel. Within a brief time the first number was sent to the schools. The paper was small, but clearly it showed the characteristics that later made it great. In 1897 the pages were so enlarged that it became possible to carry out many plans long held in abeyance. At once *Forward* became a power. Not only the young people wanted it, but parents and even pastors insisted that they must have it. The editorial page—long the product of Dr. Miller's heart and brain—was called " the best editorial

page in the country.'' It was so simple that young
people read it with delight, and so suggestive that
pastors said they found there the germ for many
of their best sermons. One reader wrote: '' I have
had more help from that editorial page than from
any other literature outside the Bible.'' This message is a fair sample of hundreds. Circulation
increased rapidly, until in 1912 more than three
hundred thousand copies were issued each week.
Editions furnished to other churches, under other
names, brought the total circulation well up toward half a million.

When the paper was enlarged, Dr. Miller told
his readers of his plans:

'' *Forward* will have its words for home life, for
school life, for social life. It will seek to help the
young people in their reading, and in their choice
of books, in their friendships, in their pleasures.
Everything that belongs to the life of a young
man or a young woman will be a proper subject
for treatment in its pages.

'' There shall be no dull pages in *Forward,* no
loose or careless writing, no light or trivial treatment of subjects, nothing sensational either in
matter or illustration, and yet the paper will be
made as bright, attractive and interesting as it
will be possible to make it.''

In a letter to a contributor he stated even more
fully his ideals.

'' No other young people's paper in the land,
with the single exception of *The Youth's Com-*

panion, reaches so many young persons, or exerts such a wide influence. It is thoroughly wholesome. It is always optimistic—not a disheartening sentence is ever admitted to its columns. Its aim is never mere entertainment—every article, every story, every briefest paragraph, to be thought worthy of publication, must have some motive of helpfulness or inspiration. The paper thus starts every week a great wave of pure, wholesome and invigorating influence which goes round the world, and makes thousands of people braver, stronger and happier, and puts into their minds higher thoughts of life's meaning, and loftier and more beautiful ideals.''

Readers of *Forward* soon learned to look on the editor as their personal friend to whom they could write freely about anything that troubled them. Once he wrote editorially of their letters:

'' The editor refers to this matter to say that nothing in all the range of his work gives him more pleasure than this personal correspondence. There is no more sacred privilege given to anyone in this world than that of helping another in some actual experience of life. The Master puts no higher honour on any of his servants than when He sends younger souls to them to be guided through some perplexing way, sorrowing ones to be comforted in their hours of grief, or tempted ones to be strengthened to endure in sin's fierce struggle. No other work which we can do for men or women is more really the very work of Christ himself than is this ministry in life's deep experiences.''

If possible every routine letter that left the office carried with it some kindly, helpful word. Contributors to *Forward* and the other periodicals learned to look for these letters, and they preserved them even when other business letters were destroyed.

One who began to write for the periodicals in 1901 has said:

" He never failed to make any business letter which he had occasion to write the opportunity for saying a kindly personal word. Once he said, ' I think of you in your work day by day, and want always to keep near you in personal thought and interest, so that if ever you need me I can know at once.' "

The receipt of articles from beginners was usually followed by the despatch of a letter of counsel and encouragement. A number of those who became valued contributors have declared that they owed their success in large part to his cheering, inspiring words.

One instance of this kind may be told at some length. In 1905 the pastor of a home mission church was compelled to resign his charge because of throat trouble. His prospects were dark. Then he began to write, and sent some of his first articles to Dr. Miller. He said nothing of his needs and his hopes, but the sympathetic editor soon learned the facts. He was not content to permit one whose letters were frequently on his desk to remain a mere name. So he wrote:

" Tell me a little about yourself sometime when you are writing, for I should like to know as much as possible about our writers.''

The information asked for was given, and the two were at once on a friendly footing.

One year many of this contributor's manuscripts were returned as unavailable. The editor detected a note of despondency in a letter which came from him just then. So he wrote:

" You must not be discouraged because sometimes stories of yours are returned. If you knew how often we have to do this in the office with our very best work, you would not have a moment for such a thought. Furnishing articles for papers is a good deal like a salesman's work in the stores —bringing goods down for the purchaser to look at. It is never expected that every piece taken down and exhibited will exactly meet the purchaser's need.''

Again this contributor was despondent because friends had been condoling with him on account of his dwindling influence: they told him it was too bad he had to give up the work of the ministry to be a mere writer for the press. Dr. Miller had just the right message for this time also:

" The assurance that words of yours have touched two millions of lives this year is a very comforting one. Some day you will know what it all means. It is a great privilege to be allowed to put touches of beauty upon immortal lives, to start impulses toward higher ideals in human hearts.''

Letters from the editor brought him more than encouragement; they were full of kindly instructions for the new work for which the minister was in training. The appreciative recipient has said:

'' Dr. Miller taught me to forget myself and to think only of my readers. He reminded me that perhaps a half or two-thirds of the readers of the Board's publications are in country places, small towns, villages, or farming districts, where their opportunities are not large, where they cannot see much of the big world nor learn what is going on, nor what the openings may be for usefulness and activity. When I had in preparation a series for *The Westminster Teacher,* he asked me to remember in writing these that the great bulk of the Sunday-school teachers who would read them would be plain people, not many of them college people, and that it was necessary, therefore, to write simply, and not upon too high a plane. He said that he had always tried to prepare all his work for persons of average intelligence, knowing that in doing this he would probably help most even those more intelligent.''

Every year, at Christmas, it was Dr. Miller's custom to send a personal letter to his contributors. These were never formal. All of his helpers expected them, and they were never disappointed.
One of the letters read thus:

"I want to thank you for the great help you have been to me during the year in your work. I need not say a word in detail about what you have done. I merely thank you for it all and assure you of sincere and most hearty appreciation.

"As the Christmas comes near my heart goes out to you in special warmth and interest. You know that your relation to me has not been merely that of a writer, but that of a personal friend. It has been a high privilege to me to stand by you through the experiences of the year, experiences of pain and sorrow, many of them, and to keep you very close to my heart in sympathy, love and prayer, all the while. I want to thank you for all that you have been to me and for what I have had the privilege of being to you.

"Let me wish for you for the Christmastide the sweetest blessings, with the gentlest revealings of Christ's grace and love in your life. May it be the best year that you ever have lived. May it bring an uplift to you, an uplift in courage, joy, strength, peace, victoriousness. May God bless you and make you very happy."

There are those who find it easier to be thoughtful of those who are far away than of those who are near at hand. This was never true of Dr. Miller. He was always most considerate and thoughtful of his editorial helpers. When he wished to see one of them, he preferred to go to that one, even if a trip into another room was necessary. If he wished the service of his stenographer, he preferred to say to her, "I have a few letters for you, if you are not too busy," rather than give her a curt direction to take his dictation. Always his associates in the office looked on him as a father and friend.

He was never too busy to plan for their comfort. On a rainy afternoon, knowing that the cars would be unusually crowded by the rush of men and women going home at five o'clock, he would frequently ask them to leave at ten minutes to five, in order that they might have seats. On a specially warm day in summer he would be apt to send out for a generous quantity of ice cream for " my editorial girls," as he called them. But his kindly interest went further than this. He entered into their lives. He knew their circumstances, and followed with interest the fortunes of other members of the household.

Although he hardly knew what it was to take a vacation, he always insisted on the period of summer rest and refreshment for the assistants. He would write them a message of good-bye as they started, they would be apt to hear from him while absent, and his welcome was sent on their return. During the summer of 1911, although himself under the care of a physician, he wrote from Atlantic City to his secretary these notes:

" I am not writing letters, but I send just this little note to assure you and your mother of loving thought these days. I hope you are both enjoying your stay at Ocean City. You are meeting lots of friends, I think. Stay as long as you can."

" This is just to welcome you back to the office. I hope you have had a good time and that both you and your mother are well."

In September, 1910, after an absence of three months caused by illness, he wrote this letter to " The Good Friends of the Editorial Department":

" I want to thank you for your faithfulness during the summer when I have been necessarily absent. I had not a moment's anxiety, knowing that you were all in your places and that every item of the work would be carefully attended to, so that nothing would be neglected or overlooked, nothing scamped. I am not surprised, therefore, to find my confidence realised and to find that everything has gone on so beautifully. I do not believe there is another editorial office in the country in which all the work is so splendidly organised, and in which the personnel of the office is so happy, so loyal to duty, so conscientious, so kindly in spirit, in every way so beautiful and worthy. No other editor could be away nearly three months as I have been and come back to find that there have been no mistakes made, no blunders, no careless performances of duty, but that all has gone on just as well as if he had been at his desk every day.

" I can only thank you, one and all, for your diligence and fidelity, and assure you of confidence and loving interest in the days to come.

" As we enter another year of work together I am sure we will be happy. I have no new requirements to exact. Let me make these simple suggestions for 1910-1911.

" We will work together in love, in patience, in kindness, in mutual thoughtfulness and helpfulness.

" We will make this the best year ever we have lived, in personal life, in habits, in character, and in our work in the office,—even surpassing our best in the past.

" We will be in our places in the office at least five minutes before nine every morning, so as to be ready for our work by nine o'clock.

" We will study our particular work and master all its smallest details, making ourselves more and more proficient, that when we have no definite assigned tasks we shall not be idle but shall ourselves find something to do that will prepare us for better usefulness.

" I cannot begin to tell you of the depth and sincerity of my interest in each one of you. I want you to let me be your personal friend. If you have any difficulty, trouble, sorrow, anxiety, or any question which you would like to bring to me, I shall always be glad to give you any cheer or help I can."

One who was his assistant for years in the editing of *Forward* told of his kindness and helpfulness in the office.

" No one could be with Dr. Miller and not be both shamed and inspired by his daily example. He was one of the quietest, simplest and humblest of workers; but his work shone out in its completeness and its ungrudgingness, and made me unsatisfied with any other kind. It was an education to work under him. He seldom criticised and he loved to praise—but a shirker

could not live in his atmosphere, just the same,
and soon faded away from the staff. Those who
remained were knit to Dr. Miller as his friends.
He was interested in their lives, and anxious to
have them reach their best.''

That Dr. Miller thought of the employees of
other departments in the large etablishment as
well as of his own was shown when in 1910 he
talked with other heads of departments of ways
to make the workers' lives brighter. As a result
of his counsel and encouragement The Westminster Club was organised by the heads of departments and their associates. Monthly meetings were arranged for. At these meetings plans
were perfected for welfare work among the employees of the Board, who then numbered nearly
one hundred. At the beginning of 1911 an opportunity was given to all employees to deposit
weekly in The Westminster Savings Fund. Thus
many were taught to save who had always spent
all they earned. The annual gathering of The
Westminster Club was made an open meeting,
when all employees were invited to a supper,
Dr. Miller and Dr. Henry, the Secretary of the
Board, being the hosts.

Dr. Miller was the first president of the club.
At the close of his term this letter of thankful
appreciation was sent to him, signed by all the
members:

'' On the occasion of our first anniversary meeting, we, the undersigned members of The West-

minster Club, wish to tell you of the joy it has been to us to have you as our first president. We feel that the helpfulness of the club has been in large measure due to your wise counsel, your constant thought, your inspiring presence. We rejoice that you have been able to meet with us so many times this year, and we are glad to look forward to other meetings when you will rejoice us by your presence.

"We thank God for the years of your service as Editorial Superintendent of the Board, and for the special privilege that has been given us of coming in touch with you in your work. Some of us do not see you very often, but the same impression is made on all of us when we do see you, we feel that we are in the presence of one whose religion is so well expressed by your own words, 'Jesus and I are friends.' By your words, by acts, by your sympathetic letters, you bring us into His presence.

"We thank you for the gift of remembrance sent us this evening. Your photograph will be a treasured possession, as your friendship is a cherished fact."

During these last years of Dr. Miller's service, when he seemed busier than ever in manifold ways, a friend asked him to tell the secret of his ability to get so much done. His answer was, "I never worry, and I try never to lose a minute." A brother editor, commenting on these words, said:

"Here was a divinely guided economist in the art of life. There was no burning of the brakes,

no overstraining of the engine, no inordinate re-
pair needed after the daily journey, but a mechanism closely geared to its work with as little
lost motion as possible, and a spirit within the
machine that was so much in fellowship with the
Spirit of God that his life was not subjected to
the terrific and sinful strain of anxious concern
over the outcome of any day. Now he did not
achieve this life course by daily struggle, but
rather by daily yielding to the daily guidance and
control of his heavenly Father.''

A briefer statement of the reason for Dr. Miller's efficiency was given by Dr. M. C. Hazard, long
editor of the Congregational Sunday School and
Publishing Society, when he said:

'' He came as near as man may to embodying
what is said about love in the thirteenth chapter of
First Corinthians. ' Love suffereth long, and is
kind; love envieth not; love vaunteth not itself,
is not puffed up, . . . seeketh not its own, . . .
taketh not account of evil; . . . believeth all
things, . . . endureth all things. Love never
faileth.' ''

HOW EDITORIAL ASSOCIATES VIEWED
HIS WORK

We are likest to Christ when we are nearest to the hearts of men, when our sympathies are widest, when we are the gentlest, when our hands are readiest to minister.—*From " One Thing I Do," in " Finding the Way."*

We do not begin to understand what our lives mean to others who see us and are touched by us. It is possible to do too much advising or exhorting of others, but we never can do too much beautiful living. One can send a blessed influence out through a whole community, just by being a splendid man. He may not be eloquent or brilliant, he may not be a statesman, an architect, a distinguished leader, a noted physician or surgeon, a gifted orator, but simply to be a worthy, noble, good man for ten, twenty, thirty years in a community, is an achievement gloriously worth while. Men who are living nobly do not begin to know how many others are living well, too, just because they are.—*From " A Call to Christian Manliness," in " The Gate Beautiful."*

CHAPTER VIII

HOW EDITORIAL ASSOCIATES VIEWED HIS WORK

When at last the unwearied worker had entered on his larger service in the world beyond, several of those who had been most intimately associated with him in his editorial work wrote of him and his achievements.

One of these was Judge Robert N. Willson, since 1889 President of the Board of Publication:

" Dr. Miller's life touched mine in more ways than one, and my association with him ran through many years. His home was for a long time directly opposite my own, and his children and mine grew up together as close neighbours and friends. The ties thus formed of personal relationship were never forgotten in the close official connection which existed between Dr. Miller and myself for many years.

".Indeed it may be said that the characteristics he displayed as a man were largely responsible for the success which came to him in his capacity as editor and writer. Sincerity, simplicity, generosity, frankness and tact were conspicuous factors in his equipment for work. He possessed a rare faculty of fairness and poise of judgment and expression in regard to matters as to which opinions differed. His industry was indefatigable, and his

devotion to the work of our Board which was entrusted to him was most marked. He was loyal to
our Church, to its doctrines and polity, and he
endeavoured with sincerity and integrity to dis-
charge his duties as editor in that spirit of loyalty.

" He had a rare faculty for collecting and re-
taining for ready use incidents, illustrations and
quotations of a simple, practical character, which
he used with great effect in his brief articles, as
well as in the books that came from his mind and
heart.

" The simplicity of his style, and the sympathy,
natural and overflowing, that was expressed by his
words, made his utterances attractive and helpful
to young and old. No religious writer of whom I
have knowledge, has ever touched the sorrowing
heart with a softer and more comforting balm than
did Dr. Miller.

" He was a great editor and a manly man. It
would have been a great mistake if anyone had in-
ferred from his mild and gentle conduct that he
was without force of character or positiveness of
opinion. These strong qualities he possessed, but
in sure control, and under the cover of a warm
heart and a kindly nature.

" Our Church, in my opinion, will never obtain
a wiser, abler or more successful editor of its
publications."

Professor W. Brenton Greene, D.D., of Princeton Seminary, chairman of the Board's Editorial
Committee, said:

" Dr. Miller was not a man to be estimated as
I would estimate myself or other men. He was in
a class by himself. I used to feel thus whenever

I contemplated the work that he did. I do not refer to his combination of the pastorate of a great church with his editorial functions or his putting himself, in addition to all this, at the unlimited disposal of anyone who needed him; but I refer simply to his editorial functions. The Sabbath-school literature of our Church, both in its extent and in its quality, literary and spiritual alike, is a monument of industry and ability that would be incredible if we had not ourselves witnessed them in operation so long as to have become accustomed to them. Yet he never seemed hurried; he was never nervous; he was never back in his work. At first I could only look on in wonder; I now look back in reverence.

"Then there was his progressiveness. Other men, as they grow older, even the best of them, drop from the head of the column. Dr. Miller never did. He died at the head of it. He was never more full of plans for the improvement of our Sabbath-school literature than during the last years of his earthly life.

"Perhaps, however, it is as a religious editor and writer that we think of him as greatest. He popularised religion in his books. Who else in our day have done it? Who of them, at all events, have done it as he did it? If we consider both the number and the sale of his books, I think that we must pronounce him the greatest religious writer of our day."

A veteran pastor and editor gave this remarkable tribute:

"The efficiency of Dr. Miller as editor and executive was highly complex in process and product, but its secret is simple. A tornado has been known to drive a soft pine board, end on, through the bole of a hardwood tree without fracture of the board. Dr. Miller's character was disciplined to compactness of fibre; but also he had accumulated the tremendous momentum of a man consciously operating ' under authority,' and thus had constantly back of him the incalculable force of the Unseen. From his early years he accustomed himself to be in vitalising, close and constant touch with God, acquiring a profound, tender and intimate sense of his presence as Father, Redeemer, Lord, Guide, Friend, Comrade and Portion. His life thus became saturated with a sense of obligation to ' redeem the time,' or as the phrase is now read, to ' buy up opportunity '; so that, automatically, waste of energy and time was eliminated. He prolonged no interview in dilatory pleasure or pause of vacancy or indecision; no speech or writing was pressed beyond due limits; prompt to begin a task, he was direct and quietly forceful in the performance, and facile in adjustment and transfer; and he always knew when to quit. No wilfulness, no selfishness, no momentary vacuity, remained perceptible among his traits so that he easily weeded out from his manner and utterance all that could hinder or offend, and thus became distinguished for noiseless and effective performance. And we must add to this his genius for friendships, which gave accumulative power to his work as organiser and leader.

" The depths of his secret are not probed until we reach the magic word, love. Probably more than any other executive of his time, his life served to redeem that word from the sentimentality, inanity and feebleness which characterise

the common notion of its meaning. With him love
was absorbed direct from God, and thus had
breadth, depth, height and scope; substance, tang
and force; the texture of polished steel; the momentum of light; the propelling power of elec-
tricity and the generative force of a great dy-
namo; directness of action like that of gravity,
with its impeccable precision; and the rhythmic
harmony of perfect machinery. ' God is love, '
and J. R. Miller was God's own child, to a very
remarkable degree reflecting the likeness and re-
producing the majestic but quiet force of Him who
is set before us as ' the express image ' of our
heavenly Father; so that in his career, somewhat
as—supremely—in that of Jesus Christ, we come
to see how practical and potent genuine love is,
how fit for harnessing to the wheels of daily life
and modern enterprise, how skilful in adjusting
effort to human machinery and providential occasion.

'' Presbyterianism has always been supposed
to be distinguished for system and intellectual
quality, and to be peculiarly hospitable to the
arts of literature; but until the year 1880 the
critical were wont to deplore a painful lack of
all this in our official publications addressed to
youth. That in 1912 this status has been re-
versed is largely due, under God, to the wisdom,
piety, skill and persistence of Dr. Miller. To
have developed either *The Westminster Teacher,*
or *Forward,* would of itself have been enough to
mark an era. To have developed the one and
created the other, to have transformed the *Visitor*
into *The Comrade* and to have developed the complete and close-jointed series of high-grade quar-
terlies which culminate in the *Teacher,* was to
bring our denomination well abreast of the times

thus far, as related to the unfolding needs of our Sunday-school work; to justify anew its reputation for weight and momentum; and thus to attach its tentacles firmly and diversely to remarkable providential opportunity as related to the training of the young in a day of growing laxity and appalling change.

" To meet the disheartening conditions due to widespread decay of family worship, home training, and catechetical instruction, to rapid absorption of unschooled masses by the Church, and to bewildering changes in forms of thcught and in educational methods, was a task to call for more of delicacy, tact, force, industry, varied knowledge, practical wisdom and executive skill than any one man could be expected to compass; yet under the leadership of Dr. Miller this has to a notable degree been effected within the bounds of our body; and it has been so effected as to organise effort for smoothly and rapidly developing the large enterprise as occasion may require in the future. Dr. Miller, in the spirit and to a remarkable degree with the skill of the Master, so shaped his labour and so impressed on it the stamp of his personality, as to pave the way for its increasing efficiency at the hands of his successors amid the unfolding conditions of the generations to come.

" This is far from all that his varied and untiring industry effected in the organic educational and literary work of the Church. His own books, and his editorial services in the book department of the Presbyterian Board of Publication, set new standards of quality and aim, addressed with kindly shrewdness to the changing conditions of thought and life. Denominational acerbities disappear under his touch. Needless frictions are abated. Truth is so presented as to seem at once weighty and winsome. Inanities, crudities, discords, clumsiness and antiquated forms cease to clog our literary machinery. Doctrinal soundness becomes wedded to an engaging manner and modern attire. The entire output of our publications is on a higher level and wears new charm. Subsoil tillage clothes worn fields of truth with living green and adorns the very roadside with fruitage and bloom. Books and periodicals become good to look at, easy to read, and no longer adulterated with materials nauseous to taste and trying to digestion. The entire work of generating an authoritative Christian literature has to a notable degree been unostentatiously rejuvenated, and infected with new vigour and attractiveness.

"How did he so accurately forecast events, show such skill in selecting assistants and associates, acquire such sanity of judgment, so fully and firmly grasp a novel and complex situation, and maintain such indomitable and diversified industry to the end? Where did he secure such singular wisdom in adjusting his methods at once to the exacting machinery of denominationalism, to the vigorous mechanism of print, publication and finance, and to the needs and appetites of his vast and inchoate public? The answer is that all this was a vital outgrowth and product. The tides of the divine life coursed freely through his spare frame, and were laboriously wrought into all his energies and capabilities. He was a man of heart, and at the same time of ideas, method, momentum and ceaseless activity. His achievements, here as in other domains of toil, are the embodiment of his spirit, his conception and his unhurried but ceaseless labour.

"He brought to his great task a life thoroughly

disciplined. He had schooled himself to be always gentle, considerate, appreciative, wary; and thus he seldom or never failed in his judgment of persons sought as associates and helpers, nor in winning and inspiring them, and in holding them steadfast. He had acquired decision of character, serenity of spirit, a persuasive winsomeness of manner, and an aromatic piety fed daily at the springs. If ' the final aim of art is to reveal the attractiveness of personality,' then Dr. Miller was a great artist. But he did not arrive at his unique power of specific and large achievement without assiduous toil reaching daily to the roots of his being. Sympathetic study of Dr. Miller, perhaps most notably in presence of his career as editor, is that most interesting and alluring thing, the study of a gracious and charming personality highly vitalised by the Spirit of God.''

A more intimate message was given by Louis F. Benson, D.D., for many years a member of the Board's Editorial Committee:

'' When I became a member of the Board of Publication, now many years ago, Dr. Miller was well started on his work as Editorial Superintendent, but had not as yet developed the periodicals and lesson helps to anything like their present proportions. His beautiful character and personality, and something of his work and writings, were of course already known to me, but I was nevertheless by no means prepared for all that I found in him, and for the remarkable development of the periodical work under his hands of which I became the witness.

" The scope of the Board's work is very wide, and few of its members can be expected to have the time and ability to cover the whole area. One has to choose the special department in which he hopes his own resources or experience can contribute something to the common stock. In this way my own attention was turned toward the periodical and book-making sides of the Board's work, and I came into very close personal and official relations with Dr. Miller.

" To know him intimately was a great privilege to any man, and such knowledge had inevitably a retroactive effect. Your heart went out to him for what he was, and in the process of admiration and affection, it became greatly enriched also. His point of view was so high, his aims were so unselfish, his methods were so self-denying, that you could not but regard them with a deep admiration and even reverence; but with them all you discovered a humility that was not a garment but a constitution. You came to feel that it was not your admiration that was being sought, nor any expression of it that was wanted, but only your sympathy in the aims and the work. Your special task was not to compliment Dr. Miller, but to try to lift yourself, for the occasion at least, to the level which with him was habitual.

" The first impression I gained of him in his official capacity was the perfect ease with which he did his work. I had indeed the feeling that he was a man larger than his sphere; though he meanwhile was already planning and preparing for the enlargement of the work to its present proportions. He was a born editor and writer, and the most indefatigable worker I have ever known. The time, pressure and the creak of the machinery in periodical work were no inconvenience or cause of nervousness. His ' thousand words ' were always ready when wanted; but their writing could at any time be suspended at the call of anyone who wanted his judgment or his help. It was, however, not the ease of his writing that was the phenomenon, but its unfailing acceptability. We have the high authority of Sir Robertson Nicoll (in *The British Weekly* for July 25, 1912) for saying that Dr. Miller may ' be justly called the most popular religious writer of his time.' We think of such a position as won by unfailing discipline of the mind, the diligent study of great models, the conscious culture of literary style. In Dr. Miller's case it seemed to be won rather by the simpler expedient of being himself and of speaking in the way natural to him. He loved others, and by loving them understood them. He addressed literally millions of people, and each one of them felt his personal touch and was conscious of the ministry of love. He had only one theme, the beauty of being better than we are. It is said that he repeated himself; and that saying probably reveals one of the secrets of his success. He was no more afraid of repeating himself than life itself is.

" Much of his work for the Board was the exposition of Scripture. It was done with a minimum of apparatus. He liked the *Cambridge Bible* best as the framework for his exposition; and it was not a learned exposition. What concerned him was the application of Scripture to life. He was not unaware of the progress of historical criticism, but his religious experience was of a character so intimate, that he felt lifted above the problems of criticism, and into that serene air he attempted to lift his readers also. Incidentally he kept the Board of Publication outside the arena of controversy in periods of some agitation in the Church.

" When he began to realise his projects for the improvement of the young people's literature and the lesson helps, he called me into innumerable conferences, and consulted me at every step. The effect, however, was to make apparent to me that he had not only editorial experience but something that may be called editorial instinct or even genius. He had nothing whatever to learn from me that could frame or modify his own decisions. I came to feel that in offering hearty coöperation, warm sympathy and earnest support to his projects, I was doing the best the circumstances of our official relations made possible. And I cherish the assurance that in that way I became something of a comfort to him. In all our relations I had never a discomfort or question, except only the abiding knowledge that he was overworked. This he never once acknowledged, and only in repeated efforts to relieve him was there any lack of coöperation on his part.

" *Forward* may stand as a monument of Dr. Miller's editorial genius; for what it is and for what it has compelled its rivals to become. It was his conception, and to his constant supervision and planning its wonderful success and influence are due. But even it does not measure his editorial capacity. He was capable of giving this country a great religious newspaper, like *The British Weekly*, and he cherished such a hope. Very often I have talked the matter over with him. Offers came to him from the outside looking toward such a project. Even within the Board of Publication the matter was discussed, but denominational restrictions made such an undertaking impracticable. The need of such a periodical remains, but I doubt if anyone can be found whose personality and gifts would bring to it the assured welcome that would have come with Dr. Miller at its head.

"Now that he is dead, more appealing even than the measure of the work he accomplished is the memory of the spirit in which he worked. One's own ideal of faithful service tends to assume a likeness to his person, and so becomes his best memorial."

THE AUTHOR OF DEVOTIONAL BOOKS

Not many of us are living at our best. We linger in the lowlands because we are afraid to climb into the mountains. The steepness and ruggedness dismay us, and so we stay in the misty valleys and do not learn the mystery of the hills. We do not know what we lose in our self-indulgence, what glory awaits us if only we had courage for the mountain climb, what blessing we should find if only we would move to the uplands of God.—*From " The Preface," in " Unto the Hills."*

We should begin now to live the immortal life, to practise immortality. We should think and plan and choose, these common days, for immortality. We should do nothing we should ever wish we had not done. We should say no words we shall ever want unsaid. We should build only fabrics we shall be glad to look upon in endless years. Immortality has begun already in the youngest life. It is not something we shall enter upon when we get to heaven. It is going on now in the schoolroom, on the playground, in the friendships and amusements of the young people, and in all their hours, however spent. We must practise immortality all our days if we would realise its fullest meaning.—*From " The Meaning of Immortality," in " The Book of Comfort."*

CHAPTER IX

THE AUTHOR OF DEVOTIONAL BOOKS

Dr. Miller's first books were prepared in answer to the clamour of those who heard his sermons on Sunday and read his helpful, stimulating articles in *The Westminster Teacher, The Sunday School Times,* and other periodicals. The first volume was issued in 1880; two final volumes from his pen were given to the public in the fall of 1912, these having been planned and prepared during his last months on earth. In all more than sixty books and booklets were issued, the total circulation during his lifetime being more than two million copies. Not only were they in demand in America and Great Britain, and all the colonies, but in other foreign lands as well. One or more volumes have been translated into German, French, Italian and Norwegian. The claim made by his publishers that Dr. Miller is " the most widely read devotional writer in the world " is well founded.

The reason for this popularity was easily seen by anyone who knew him and his methods of work. During the week he lived close to people. He saw them in their homes and in his office and entered into the deepest secrets of their hearts. On Saturday afternoon and evening he thought over the week, and prepared his sermons for Sunday. On Sunday he gave his people messages that reached their hearts because they were prepared with a sympathetic knowledge of their needs. On Monday, from the sermons of Sunday, articles would be written for the papers. Almost at once after publication messages would begin to come from those who had been helped by reading them. In a few months a new volume would be made up by revising and rewriting the articles which had already served double duty. This volume would not be long out of the publishers' hands before—from all parts of the world—letters would pour in from readers. Many of these letters would bring heart-revelations that inspired fresh sermons and articles and books.

The sermons that adapt themselves to publication as newspaper articles and then for insertion in books for popular reading are scarce. But Dr. Miller could write them—in fact, he seemed unable to write any other kind. Long discipline in writing simply, and long and varied experience in loving men, women and children fitted him to be author of more " best sellers " among religious books than anyone else.

Simple writing was a hobby with him. To an associate in the editorial office he once said, " I would like to see you make these articles so simple that an eight-year-old child cannot but understand them." His work showed how completely he had kept this ideal before his own mind. One whose business it was to estimate the space required for manuscripts by various authors, soon learned that a thousand words by Dr. Miller would need one-fifth less space than one thousand words by almost any other writer—all because he was so fond of words of one syllable! Simple language was illuminated by apt and copious illustration. Many of his illustrations were given in a single sentence. Most of these were illustrations that no other writer would ever have used—because they were drawn from homely life, and because they were so simple that no one else thought of the application that was so plain to Dr. Miller. Yet no sooner did he use them than they were copied by numerous other authors and used in sermons everywhere.

A reader of Dr. Miller's books discovers that in every chapter, sooner or later, he says something comforting. This characteristic was noticeable during the days of the Civil War, when the papers printed his first messages. Letters from the front were apt to contain a message of cheer. When he could get time he would write a full article on the one theme that took possession of him as he went to hospital cots or to soldiers dying on the battle field, or as he came in touch with grieving parents. In 1863 he wrote to *The United Presbyterian* " A Study on Sorrow," in which he said:

" I had spent the afternoon of Wednesday with two or three sore sufferers. In conversation with them I had spoken freely of their trials and their comforts. . . . Comfort is one of life's best blessings. Even the comfort of earthly friends is soothing and sweet. But the real comfort which the Holy Spirit brings to the heart of the Christian mourner is infinitely better. . . . It is better to go into the furnace and get the image of Christ out of the fire, than to be saved from the fire and fail of the blessed likeness."

Another war-time article, entitled " A Word of Comfort," contained this illustration:

" When a hard frost comes after a rain it catches the silvery drops that fasten upon the trees, and freezes them solid, and holds them there in beautiful crystals which no wind can shake off. So death catches all the beauty and sweetness of those we love and fixes it in solid crystals which will hang upon the tree of memory forever."

The titles of some of the books published a generation or more after the close of the war show plainly that the passing years only intensified the feeling of the young Field Agent that the world needs comforting words. As one reads the list of Dr. Miller's works he is at once attracted by such refreshing titles as " Silent Times," " Come Ye Apart," " Bits of Pasture," " The Hidden Life," " The Blessing of Cheerfulness," " By the Still Waters," " Strength and Beauty," " The Ministry of Comfort," " Upper Currents," " In Perfect Peace." No one was surprised to learn that the last book of the Silent Times series, and the last book prepared by Dr. Miller for publication, was entitled simply " The Book of Comfort." *

To one who spoke of the constant recurrence of the comforting, soothing note in his sermons, Dr. Miller once said, " I have long made it a rule never to preach one sermon on any subject without putting in it, somewhere, a message of comfort for the sorrowing and the overborne." And to one who commended his books he wrote words that told the secret of his life:

" You speak specially of the uplifting influence, the cheering and encouraging tone of my work. I feel that it is one of the highest missions of the Christian teacher to be an inspirer of others. Enough people write the sad words, the depressing words, which make life heavier and harder for those who are meeting its responsibilities and enduring its struggles. Those who sing always in a minor key, and breathe out sad and dispiriting words, do not know how much harm they are doing in the world, what hurt they are giving to other lives. It seems to me that those who know Christ should sing the note of gladness and joy. Life is sad enough even at its best. As we go forth each morning we meet on every hand those whose hearts are burdened, who are carrying heavy loads, who find the battle too sore for them. If we speak discouraging words or if we even refrain from speaking glad and joyous words, we are making life a little harder for those

* Published in England under the title, " Life's Open Doors."

people. But if we have in our hearts the cheer
of Christ, the encouragement of Christ, we shall
be all the better helpers of others. I have been
greatly impressed by a word in the prophecy of
Isaiah, referring to the Messiah, in which the
prophet says, ' He shall not fail nor be discouraged.' As you study the life of Christ you find
that He never was discouraged. All His days He
met life's trials and persecutions and sorrows with
a shining face and a courageous heart. I never believed that old tradition which said that He never
smiled—I believe that on His face there was always that sweet smile which told of peace within.
It is our duty, therefore, as far as we possibly can,
to be encouragers of others, never discouragers.''

Everywhere the critics received Dr. Miller's volumes kindly. A writer in the Edinburgh *Expository Times* said of " A Help for the Common
Days '':

" It is a work that for a moment may be con-
founded with ————'s [naming a famous devotional writer]. It is really quite distinct. ————
at his best mounts up with wings as eagles. Dr.
Miller is always at his best, and always is content
to walk. And this is no disparagement of Dr.
Miller. If we may believe Principal Reynolds,
this steady upward plodding in a narrow path is
better than raptures of reconciliation. Therefore
for strength in daily duty, the duty of patient,
silent waiting for the slow ' grinding of the mills
of God,' we shall seek Dr. Miller.''

A well-known American critic said of " The
Building of Character '':

" It has the charming simplicity of all your work. You have the rare art of saying things clearly, effectively, tenderly, applicatorily, and yet without the air of a pedagogue and without the tone of preachment."

But the best critics are those who buy and read books. These were not slow to express themselves about Dr. Miller's work. Nearly every morning's mail brought one or more notes of appreciation from some one who had been helped by a volume of comfort, or inspired to nobler living by a message prepared by one who was learning the lesson of life in the school of his Friend Jesus Christ. Sometimes praise was laughingly given, as when a father wrote that his daughters had a good-natured dispute every evening as to who should have the great privilege of reading a chapter in the latest volume, or when one told that a boy, asked if he was fond of a certain popular book of adventure, said, " Yes, it means as much to me as the last of Dr. Miller's books means to mother."

Perhaps one of the best criticisms of Dr. Miller's books ever made came from a humble reader in England:

" It does seem to me the most wonderful thing in the world, when I consider your high standing and the many calls upon your time, that you should be so kind to me and give me so much of your help and thought. Do you know I think God must have meant you to be my teacher, because I can understand you so quickly and because it is such an intense joy to learn from you. I have been reading Emerson's Essays lately and like them very much, but not at all in the same way I like your books; for when I read Emerson I am at school; when I read your books I am resting at home.''

In the same mail would come letters from readers at home and from readers beyond the sea. One day a message from the homeland said:

'' I have for twenty years been an invalid, and have had so many solitary hours, so many silent times, when the companionship of your books was comforting, inspiring and uplifting, that I love them.''

Another letter told of an evening gathering of men and women in a home for the aged to listen to the reading aloud of selected books. One of the listeners said:

'' Nothing which has passed through our hands has been so acceptable as ' Finding the Way.' ''

From Melbourne, Australia, came a letter from a Christian Endeavourer who told of the purpose of his society to spend '' An Evening with Dr. Miller.''

The English Consul at Kieff, Russia, told of a service held in the schoolhouse every Sunday afternoon for several years, at which a chapter from one of Dr. Miller's books was read. No sermon was allowed by the authorities, but the printed words of the American pastor met their needs.

From a stranger in London, England, came these encouraging tidings:

" A friend, an architect in Bombay, India, informs me that at Christmas he purchased three hundred copies of your ' Come Ye Apart ' and distributed them among his friends and native clients. One of them went to a Mohammedan prince, for whom he had recently constructed a palace and in whose house he had great freedom. He afterwards said that the volume was being read with much interest both by the prince and his wife. Another copy was sent to a Mohammedan merchant, and on calling at his office the giver found the book lying on the table, it having been brought from the residence. I thought you would like to know of these silent influences at work."

Famous people asked to have their part in the chorus of appreciation. From Hawarden Castle came an autograph letter:

" Pray accept my thanks for your work on ' The Building of Character.' It seems to me a work of great value on a subject requiring a skilful hand.
          " Your very faithful servant,
                    " W. E. GLADSTONE."

The Earl of Meath wrote from England:

" I have for some considerable time wished to write to you and express the pleasure which I feel in reading your books. I think I may truly say that they are the only sermons which have ever attracted me. Yours possess a life and practical character which appeal to me, and I seldom read them without feeling that I rise strengthened for life's contests. They appear to me so different from the ordinary dry-as-dust sermons, which treat of abstruse questions of theology or contested points of the Bible narrative, which are of little practical use to the man of the world who is in need of guidance as to the way in which he should pick his steps amidst the dangers and pitfalls to be daily met with in the workaday world. Permit, therefore, an unknown friend to tender sincere thanks for guidance and encouragement.''

A Philadelphia visitor to the palace of the Czar in St. Petersburg wrote that he saw several of Dr. Miller's books on the reading table of the Czarina. She asked him to say to the author that she had read his books and enjoyed them very much. Later she sent a similar message through her secretary.

Gratifying as were these evidences that he was reaching the hearts of the great, the author welcomed even more the words that came to him from those in humble station. When in San Francisco, in 1893, Dr. Miller visited the Chinese Quarter. Going into one of the houses, he was introduced to the owner, who showed the greatest delight on meeting him, and exclaimed, " Why, I know you well; I have read your books! " and going to a table near by he held up several of them.

Dr. Miller was particularly attracted by this

letter, received from a student at the University of Mississippi:

" Last summer a party of us students were over in South Carolina working during vacation to help get into school again. In the library of my boarding house a little volume in green binding attracted my attention. It was your ' Week-day Religion.' I not only read the book myself, but read it aloud to my friends. We ordered copies at once, and more than one of us, I suspect, had copies sent to some dark-eyed maiden in the old Magnolia state. I have the book on my table now, and in the hurry and grind I take time to read it even though I have read it again and again. Its simple and sweet earnestness goes straight to my soul. You are a busy man in far-away Philadelphia, and I a farmer's boy and student among the vine-clad hills of Mississippi, yet I know that we are drawn close together by that greatest of all ties—the recognition of our duty to Christ."

A young negro minister in the South evidently spoke from his heart when he said:

" While at the seminary I got a plenty of doctrine, but little of practical things, little of words suited to cheer the weary and heavy-hearted, but in your books I find many things that are good for the sufferings of my race. And I thank God for your life."

The day before the author's death a maid-servant in England wrote:

" I want to try in writing to thank you for the great help I have received from reading books

written by you, namely: ' Silent Times Series.'
I have had the great privilege of being able to
read and re-read, for years now, some of these.
I find in counting up that I have read seventeen
of the most beautiful and helpful books. Again
and again I have thanked God for placing them
within my reach. Again and again I have asked
Him to reward you, though at the same time I
know you have had already your reward. I cannot express in words my heartfelt thanks for the
help I have received from them, and the joy it
has given me to be able to lend to others the three
volumes I possess as my own. I would like to
have every one you have written as my very own.
I hope yet to be able to read those I have not
read. I am a domestic servant and, you will understand, not well enough off to purchase them all
for my own. But my mistress is as fond of them
as I am, and it is through her kindness that I
own three of them. For some time I have felt
I would like to thank you, and I didn't know if
you were in heaven above or in heaven below, for
I know after being able to write such books, you
must have known the blessed experience of heaven
on earth. So I inquired of the publishers and
they sent me your address. Dear Sir, please accept again my sincere gratitude for those books.
I pray that millions of them may be bought, and
I know they cannot fail to be a blessing to all who
read them. I say all, because I believe no one
who is saved can read them without being blessed.
Some day, when I meet the blessed Master, I will
thank Him face to face, and you, too.''

Many letters told of lives that had been changed
by God's blessing on these simple volumes. A
useful minister said:

" Dr. Miller's fine spiritual articles and editorials have often inspired me to higher living and greater devotion to the cross. One of his little books, ' Go Forward,' helped me to determine a field of labour in harmony with the will of God. Had I not read it at the time, I might have gone to the other field."

One who became an earnest Christian after the experience described in his letter, wrote:

" When I took the book up, I was in utter despair. I had been longing for over a year to become a Christian, but had been unsuccessful, and had almost determined to give up the struggle. When I laid down the book all my miserable doubts and fears had vanished, and I was so perfectly happy that I doubted the reality of the change. Not until two or three years had passed did I dare to believe in my new peace."

An anxious mother cheered the author by saying:

" I have thrown ' The Every Day of Life ' in the way of my son, who is rather careless about reading such books, and I am glad to tell you I often find him reading it. And only this morning at breakfast, when we were talking about the book, he remarked, ' I tell you, Dr. Miller is a great man. He knows how to say things that go to the heart.' . . . Last night I received a letter from a young man, thanking me for a copy of the book which I had sent him, and expressing a desire to lead a new life."

From a deaconess in Toronto, Canada, came this encouraging note:

" Your books have been my favourites for years, and I have been echoing their helpful messages to all my patients in the seven hospitals of the city where my work calls me day by day; and also in our young people's meetings. I have come in from my work with my heart almost crushed with the sorrows and miseries of this wicked world, but would pick up one of your books, and it would give me just the message I needed for the hour. . . . A good friend was kind enough to say to me the other evening, ' I know now the secret of your unselfish life; it is because you have read so many of Dr. Miller's books.' I want to say to you that they have helped me to get better acquainted with Christ."

It was one of Dr. Miller's chief joys that his books were acceptable to people of all denominations and all phases of belief. He prized highly a letter written in 1887 by Bishop William Bacon Stevens, of the Protestant Episcopal Diocese of Pennsylvania. After receiving " Practical Religion," the Bishop wrote:

" Pardon me for thus writing to a stranger; and yet I feel that where our minds and hearts so run together, and find their common centre in the same precious Saviour, we are not strangers, but brethren in Christ, journeying, though it may be by different paths, yet each leading to the same Gate of Pearl, and to the one Father's house, of whom ' the whole family in heaven and earth is named.' "

On returning from a vacation trip a Philadelphian said:

" While stopping at a hotel on one of the islands in beautiful Casco Bay, the proprietress inquired whether I was acquainted with Dr. Miller. I was surprised at her question, because I knew her to be a member of the Roman Catholic Church. ' I always have one of Dr. Miller's books with me wherever I may happen to be,' she explained. ' His words have comforted me in my sorrow and helped me more than any others I have ever read; he seems almost to know my problems, and in his books I have found a way out of many difficulties.' Then she added, ' I was advised to get Dr. Miller's books by the priest in charge of my church.' "

A Roman Catholic Archbishop was heard by the proprietor of a bookstore talking to a parish priest. He said: " Here is a book that I like. It is by J. R. Miller. I do not know who he is, but it is a good book and I advise you to read it."

Dr. Miller's friends were not surprised by letters of praise and appreciation like these. But Dr. Miller was surprised. He never got over the feeling expressed in a letter to a friend:

" I thank you for what you say about the influence of my articles and books on the other side of the sea. It is something which I cannot myself understand—how the books go and how kindly people write to me. This morning's mail brought me two letters—one from Southern India and another from England, both full of grateful thanks, out of loving hearts, for the simple words which God has enabled me to write. Nothing humbles a man so much as the consciousness that God is using him. The feeling of reverence which one has in such consciousness, instead of exalting, brings one down very close to the feet of Christ.''

In similar vein he wrote to another correspondent:

'' There is something pleasant about the way my books have gone. I confess myself mystified when I think of it. The sales on the other side, through my British publishers, are quite as great as on this side. God has chosen to use these little books with their simple messages in a way which no thought of mine can understand or account for. The only solution I can find is that God graciously accepts the little things laid on His altar and uses them as He wills, to carry comfort, cheer, inspiration and help to His children.''

In 1893, after a Sunday in Oakland, California, where the people had thronged about him, he wrote to Mrs. Miller:

'' I am getting little glimpses of the place I hold in the people's hearts over the country through books, articles, lessons, etc. People say in their introductory speeches that my ' name is a household word.' One stranger said that no man in this country has the place I have in the hearts of the Christian people. I feel silly to write this, as it seems like self-conceit. But you say I ought to tell you everything. It does not make me self-conceited at all, but just the reverse. It gives me a sense of responsibility which will make me far more careful of my life hereafter.''

Strong in that resolution, the gifted author returned to his desk to prepare fresh messages of comfort and stimulus for the friends of his Friend and those he would introduce to that Friend.

MINISTERING THROUGH THE MAILS

If you know a life that is dreary, that seems utterly desolate and alone, do what you can to get a bit of bloom planted in it.—*From "Upper Currents."*

Jesus never gave money to anyone in need, so far as we are told. He did not pay rents for the poor, nor buy them food or clothes, but he was always doing good in ways that meant far more to them than if he had helped with money. There are needs that only love and kindness can meet. Countless people move about among us these days starving for love, dying for loneliness. You can help them immeasurably by becoming their friend, not in any marked or unusual way, but by doing them a simple kindness, by showing a little human interest in them, by turning aside to do a little favour, by manifesting sympathy, if they are in sorrow. A little note of a few lines sent to a neighbour in grief has been known to start an influence of comfort and strength that could not be measured.

It is the little things of love that count in such ministry—the little nameless acts, the small words of gentleness, the looks that tell of interest and care and sympathy. Life is hard for many people and nothing is more needed continually than encouragement and cheer. There are men who never do anything great in their lives, and yet they make it sunnier all about them and make all who know them happier, braver, stronger. There are women, overburdened themselves, perhaps, but so thoughtful, so sympathetic, so obliging, so full of little kindnesses, that they make the spot of the world in which they live more like heaven.—*From "Comfort Through Personal Helpfulness," in "The Book of Comfort."*

CHAPTER X

MINISTERING THROUGH THE MAILS

DR. MILLER built up his large congregations as much by letter-writing as by the making of personal calls. And the letters which played such an important part in the development of his work were not about the church at all—they were merely the friendly, thoughtful, considerate letters of one who was interested in the welfare of his correspondents and who did not allow himself to be too busy to let them know about his interest.

For years it was his habit on Sunday evenings, after the day's work was done, to make note of all the people of whom he had heard during the day to whom letters might do good. Of course the names of the sick went down on that list, as well as those who had recovered from sickness, those who had returned from a journey, and those who were about to leave home; those who were going to college, or parents who had heard good news from a son or a daughter at college—in fact, everyone into whose life had come some event of special importance. Just as soon as possible, a letter was sent to each one of them, with an appropriate word of sympathy, congratulation, cheer, or good wishes.

Then he kept a complete record of all the important dates in the lives of his people—birthdays, wedding anniversaries, et cetera—and he marked each of these by sending a short letter of remembrance.

As if this was not enough, when he heard from acquaintances during the week of sickness or death in a family with which he was acquainted—whether in his own town or in distant parts of America, or even in foreign countries—he seized the chance to write a letter. In fact, it was the rule of his life to send each day at least one letter of cheer to some one who was in special need. Seldom, however, did he stop with one such letter; the day's mail from his office was frequently loaded with a dozen or more messages of cheer. The chance word with the street-car conductor, or the passenger who sat by his side, or the elevator boy, or the teller at the bank would give him the hint that prompted a message. Perhaps the morning paper would tell him of some one who had been called to a position of honour, possibly a caller would casually mention the fact that a friend had just been married. A business associate might tell him of one who had recently come to the city to enter upon a new position. Notes would be made of each of these opportunities for a helpful letter —and before the day was done the message was on its way.

Once when he was present as a speaker at an evening gathering he learned that two expected guests had been unable to come because of illness. Quickly his memorandum book was in his hand, the fact was noted, and at the first opportunity he wrote letters of sympathy to both of the men. It made no difference to him that one was obscure, while the other was a man of note: the obscure man received a letter just as hearty as that penned for the well-known man.

During the Torrey-Alexander meetings in Philadelphia in 1906, a service was held in the Academy of Music, conducted by Charles M. Alexander. Different persons were testifying to their faith in Christ and relating experiences which had led them to accept Him. One of these persons spoke of the influence of a letter received from Dr. Miller in a time of deep trouble and distress. " Yes," said Mr. Alexander, " what a wonderful help Dr. Miller's letters have been to many a weary and troubled soul! I wonder how many persons in this gathering have received letters from Dr. Miller? " One might have expected to see a scattering show of hands here and there throughout the large congregation, but hundreds of hands were raised in silent but eloquent tribute to a man who, although extremely busy, found time to share the burdens of others.

Once a visitor told Dr. Miller what one of these kindly letters had meant to him. Dr. Miller told the story himself in an article urging others to write such letters. It never occurred to him that friends would know at once that he wrote the letter of which the young man spoke. This is the story, with Dr. Miller's own comment:

" Only yesterday a young man took from his pocket a letter which he had carried for five years and which he has read no doubt hundreds of times. It was written when he was in great perplexity of mind and was on the point of turning into the darkness of doubt and despair. He reached out his hands for help, writing to one he knew he could trust, and laying bare to him his heart's whole burden. He received a prompt answer which, if it did nothing else, at least brought to him the consciousness of human sympathy and interest. He was not alone. One cared for him. For the time, in the darkness, he could not see Christ, but he could see this human friend who stood close by him in love. This saved him. This friendship was a little lamp which kept on shining when every other light seemed to have gone out.

" The letter which came to him in answer to his heart's unburdening proved the very word of Christ to him. For months it was all the gospel he could read. Its few, strong, simple, confident sentences were like anchor-chains to his soul amid the waves. At last all the darkness fled away, the storms were quieted, Christ himself was revealed once more in blessed, glorious light, and holy peace filled his soul.

" But it was the letter that saved him. It was the hand of Christ to him. Is it any wonder that he cherished it as the most sacred of all his treasures? It has been kept so long and read so often that the paper is worn out. But no money would buy it from the young man."

In homes all over the world letters from Dr. Miller are cherished possessions. A visitor in a New Jersey home was shown a series of seven letters received from him on seven successive wedding anniversaries. Most people would have thought the recipients had no claim on him, but he thought differently; everyone had a claim to whom he might be of use.

" I can't understand how he could keep in touch with folks as he did," a business man said a few days after the death of the letter-writer. " I have carefully laid away a package of messages from him. Somehow he kept track of me from the time I took my first position. Every time my salary was increased he wrote to me. There was a letter when I was married, and more letters on wedding anniversaries. When a child was born, when there was sickness in the home, when there were financial reverses, when we were rejoicing or sorrowing for almost any special reason, he wrote to us. And to think that he did no more for us than for thousands of others, some of whom he had never seen."

A few samples of these letters serve not only to illustrate the story of the writer's helpful ministry of the pen, but they reveal many of the secrets of his marvellous life. One day a letter came to his desk from a Sunday-school girl who asked for counsel as to her life work. After urging patience before beginning the larger work she planned, he wrote:

"I am glad to know that you have given yourself to Christ fully and wholly, that you desire not only to live for Him, but to live to be a blessing to others in His name. . . . Your best course is to put yourself in the hands of Christ, as I am sure you want to do, not only regarding the consecration of the work, but regarding the details of the work. Do not be in haste. Do not feel that you must enter at once upon this larger work. The first thing for a worker is careful and substantial preparation. Meanwhile you will not be idle, but you will be doing Christ's work and taking a part in Christian work from the very beginning. You will practise, for example, in Sunday-school work and in every line of work in which girls can engage with helpfulness to others. Let Christ choose the way and choose the line of work for you. I have had experience with a good many young people who have felt just as you feel now, having the beautiful spirit of consecration and great earnestness, and I assure you that the course I recommend will be the wise one for you—not to be in a hurry, but to do the work of this day faithfully as a preparation for the work of the morrow."

A student for the ministry, about to be graduated from college, received this stimulating counsel:

"May God's blessing richly abide upon you in the future plans for the completion of your course. The seminary curriculum will be different altogether from that of the college. You are in a measure free from the trammels and drudgeries which have been thus far an essential part of your course. The work before you now is twofold—first, to get the keys of the treasure house of knowledge, which will make available to you the rich stores which are laid up for your use; and, second, to learn to preach. A man must have something to say, otherwise rhetoric and elocution and all other such qualifications for expression will be of little avail. The day has gone by when sounding brass and tinkling cymbal will make a man a permanent reputation in the pulpit, or enable him to be of much use in the world. There was a time when high-sounding rhetoric and graceful oratory took the place largely with many people of real thought. But now a man must know something, must have something to say to people, must be a thinker, otherwise he will find his rhetoric and elocution of but very small importance. It is impossible for you in the three years before you to learn everything that you will need to use in your ministry. But you can get the keys to the storehouse. That is, you can learn where things are to be found, and you can learn how to think. Reading alone does not prepare a man for being a great teacher. He must not only read, but also digest and assimilate.

" The other part of your course will be to learn to express what you do know in such a way that it will leave its mark in the hearts and lives of those who hear you. Nothing will be of more use to you than incessant writing. No matter how stiffly and laboriously a man may write at first, if only he persists in practice, writing every day, rewriting and striving to improve in his style, he will by and by be able to express his thoughts fluently and in such a way that others will be interested in the expression. Elocution is important, but I insist still that the men who move the world and make the deepest impression upon lives are those who have learned to write in simple Saxon words of beauty and strength, the great thoughts that burn in their hearts.''

A Christian in another city on the morning of his birthday read this greeting:

'' I have just seen a notice in the New York *Evangelist* that to-morrow will be your birthday. I am constrained to write a word of sincere congratulation. There are many things upon which you are to be congratulated. One is, that through the grace of Christ in you, your life has been such a blessing to the world, so full of usefulness, such an educating, uplifting influence. You will never know the full value of what you have done until in eternity you see all the results and inspirations when the harvest is gathered. . . .

'' Another cause for congratulation is that you have an immortality before you, bright with possibilities of growth, in which you are going to continue to work for Christ. This is the best of all. The ' endless life ' beyond the shadows of mortality is a great deal more real than the broken years we live in this world. There the oldest are the youngest and all life is toward youth.

'' May God continue you for many years of usefulness here, and then introduce you to an eternity of glorious life.''

A letter from a stranger attracted Dr. Miller's special attention because it gave him the hint for which he was always looking—the hint that a letter from him would be helpful. So he wrote:

'' Your stationery shows that you are in sorrow. I may not intermeddle with your grief, but

I may say at least that my heart goes out in sincere sympathy to you, whatever the grief may be which has touched your life. No doubt you have learned that sorrow is a great revealer. We never should see the stars in the sky, if the sun kept shining always; and the Bible is like a sky full of stars—stars of comfort, of divine revealing, of spiritual help, of which we never should know experimentally did not the sun go down for us and the darkness come on. Very much of the Bible remains like a sealed book to God's children until they are called to pass into the shadows of grief. That is what our Master meant in the Beatitude for sorrow, ' Blessed are they that mourn, for they shall be comforted.' Comfort is one of God's highest and best blessings. But we never can have comfort till we mourn.''

A young woman who was just entering on her service as governess in a private family was strengthened thus:

'' My child, do not be afraid of your new duties and responsibilities. Keep near the heart of Christ yourself, for there you will receive strength, and your life will be enriched and your touch made more gentle and your heart made more tender. Your duties are new to you and may not be very easy, but I hope you will soon get accustomed to them. It is a great thing to be able to put an inspiration of good or beauty into the heart of a child. You never can know what the final outcome will be. May God bless you always.''

Learning that an acquaintance was about to lose a position through the suspension of a business house, he entrusted to the mails these heartening sentences:

" May God bless you. You must not be afraid. You have come to one of those points in life where you must call up the resources of your Christian faith. You will find in due time that the things you have been saying to other people are true. God will not forget you. He has some plan for your life and some place for you to work, and He would not be your Father if He did not mean to guide you to the place and to the work in due time."

On one of the anniversaries of a great sorrow which had come into the life of a friend, he took this way to ease the wound which would be opened anew by the day:

" I sympathise with you in the feeling of lone-liness of which you speak. Anniversary days and vacation times are the hardest periods through which to pass in time of loneliness. They bring back the memories of other resting days and me-morial days when you were not alone. But these very experiences which try you so much are bring-ing you two blessings. First they are showing to you the value of strong human friendships, whose worth to you you would probably never have realised but for these experiences. Then at the same time they are making known to you the reality of God's help and mercy. I often say we get a new Bible in our time of trouble, just as a person gets a new sky when the sun goes down. During the day the sky is only blue—beautiful, rich, deep in its majesty and serenity, but not revealing all of its splendours until night comes. Then in the darkness the glory of the stars flashes out. So it is with the Bible. You know it, you read it, you love it, you feast your heart upon its promises, even in the days of joy and human friendship. But you have not yet seen its best. Shades of night come on, and in the darkness the promises flash out with all their tender meaning and all their strength and helpfulness.''

A young soldier enlisted for the Spanish War was in the midst of peculiar temptations. He was held back from vicious courses as he read these words:

'' I am sure you want to be a true man as well as a true Christian. I hope that nothing will lead you away from loyalty to Christ. I am sure you mean to be true, but I know well the temptations of a soldier's life, for I spent three years in the army during our Civil War. I know many men who were not able to withstand the temptations. But I know thousands of others who were made better men by the temptations because they met them bravely and were faithful. I hope that you will belong to the latter class. You have your life to live, and you must be a man not only successful in a worldly sense, but also respected by your fellow men and beloved by all good people. You are now at school—these many days will test your character and bring out whatever is best in you, if only you are loyal and true. Stand like a rock therefore. You have given yourself to Christ, standing up before the whole congregation saying, ' I am a Christian and I will be faithful to my Master while I live.' You want to be a brave soldier when you stand in the face of danger; it is far more important that you should be a brave man, standing true to God in the face of all the temptations that you meet.''

One who reads these letters is ready to agree to the truth of an illuminating sentence contained in a missive to one who was struggling with doubts:

'' To me religion can all be expressed in one little line, ' Jesus and I are friends.' That is my creed.''

Of course Dr. Miller's daily mail was full of answering letters from those privileged to receive the wonderful messages of counsel and help. One day this came from a weary minister whose heart was weighted with woe:

'' Your note is like a breath from the balsams, bringing refreshment and cheer to my dear suffering wife and to me. Now and then when riding to my appointments when I was a country pastor in eastern North Carolina, I used to come suddenly upon a little stretch of road which was made fragrant by the yellow jasmine, or bay. Your letter reminds me of such an experience, and I thank you with all my heart.''

One whom Dr. Miller had encouraged in his struggle to secure an education against odds wrote, years after his graduation:

'' Just a line to express my deep gratitude for all that you have been to me during the years that have elapsed since we first met. In going over my effects I found letters of encouragement from you at the completion of my college and seminary career, and letters of cheer to greet a homesick boy arriving at Salt Lake City. In fact there were no experiences of joy or sorrow that met me that you did not share with me. I have treasured these letters all these years.

" What little good I have done in the Master's cause is largely due to the stimulus of your influence."

On learning of the sudden death of a missionary, Dr. Miller wrote at once to the parents, although he had never met them. Not long after he received grateful acknowledgment from the father:

" I write, thanking you for your most cordial, timely and useful letter of condolence. It comforted both of us. Your allusions and illustrations were, as customary with you, most apt and telling. We have, in fact, felt more exultation and deep joy than grief, in hearing of our son's work, and its triumphant close—on earth. Your letter, so prompt, apt and extended, and from a source more appealing to us than you could know, went far to confirm and heighten in us the feelings named. That you could find time to write it, and that you took the time and thought, meant much to us, and lent emphasis to your kind and wise words. You doubtless do not need this response as an encouragement to like future ministries to others, but the circumstances forbid our silence: you ought to be told, sometimes, what flavour God lends to your words, and thus what power they carry for good."

The passion for writing letters continued to the last. One day in May, 1912, while unable to leave his chair, Dr. Miller dictated letters to a minister who was celebrating the fiftieth anniversary of his pastorate, to a young man who was that day moving into his new home, to a sick friend, and to a man who had just been highly honoured. His last letter—written several weeks before his death—was a message of appreciation to an associate. He was so feeble that he fell asleep several times before the letter was completed, but he would not give up. He had thoroughly learned that

> " Just the art of being kind
> Is all the great world needs."

He had learned this lesson from his Friend. And tens of thousands have been the richer because of his desire to pass on what his Friend had taught him.

THE WORLD HIS PARISH

God is always sending people to us in providential ways. We do not know why they came to us, why they pass within the range of our influence. But in whatever way they are sent to us we have some errand to them. They may need our sympathy, our encouragement, our comfort, our protection, the influence of our friendship. Let us be careful lest while we are busy here and there they are gone without having received the influence which God intended us to give them.—*From "The Work of the Lord," in "The Gate Beautiful."*

We may do the peacemaker's work by seeking always to bring together those who have been estranged. In every community there are such persons. Sometimes they live under the same roof and eat at the same table. There are brothers and sisters, there are even husbands and wives, who are further apart than any strangers. A thick wall of rock has been built up between them. It may be difficult to do anything to heal such estrangements. But even in the most unhappy and most hopeless alienations the peacemaker's holy work may yet be crowned with success.—*From "On Being a Peacemaker," in "A Heart Garden."*

There are some whose lives are so set apart for ministry to others and so filled with calls for service that they seem to have no opportunity to be ministered to by others. They are always giving and never receiving. They spend their days in helping others, but no one helps them. They carry the burdens of many, but no one comes to carry their burden. They are comforters of the sorrow of all their friends, but in their own grief no one ministers consolation to them. They share their bread with the hungry, but when they are hungry no man gives unto them. Yet these find their help in the very serving to which they devote their lives. In feeding others, they are fed. In comforting others, they are comforted. In blessing others they are blessed. It matters not that no others come to serve them—they are served in their service.—*From "Getting Help from People," in "Upper Currents."*

CHAPTER XI

THE WORLD HIS PARISH

DURING the last year of his life Dr. Miller wrote
what was—for him—an unusually personal message to one who sought to know his idea of consecration. He wrote:

" I have regarded myself as reaching the most
real things of Christian life and privilege when I
have let Christ possess me wholly, living in me
and through me. I have felt that my work is
simply to interpret Christ to others, to let Christ's
love pour out through my love, to let Christ's
cheer for others voice itself through my words,
and to live out as far as I can the unselfishness
of Christ in self-forgetful service of others. In-
creasingly, during recent years, God has been
trusting me with the helping of hundreds and
thousands of people. He has sent them to me
that I may do for them what the Master Himself
would do for them if He were here in the flesh.
He is here in the flesh to me, and in a small degree, at least, I am to let Him live in me and live
through me. Persons come to me for advice and
for guidance and for comfort and for help in almost every experience, and for rescue, ofttimes
when it seems almost to be impossible. Increas-
ingly, also, I have found that God is ready to use
me for the helping of those who come to me, sometimes in almost startling ways. The real answer-

ing of prayers in a great many cases has been something that has awed me."

In "letting Christ's love pour out" through his love he made no distinctions among people. No matter who they were, or where they lived, if they needed the help he could give, to them was help to be given. When he was asked to conduct a funeral service a favourable answer did not depend on the fact that the family worshipped with the congregation of which he was pastor; he attended scores of funerals in the homes of total strangers. Especially in the summer when other ministers were away on vacation he answered calls from members of many churches and from members of no church.

So it was with his calls on the sick and the sorrowing, he was at the service of anyone and everyone. Once a woman asked him to visit her daughter who was dying of consumption. "She heard you pray in the house of a friend, and she wants you," was the explanation. "We are Catholics, but that won't make any difference, will it?"

One day a stranger asked him if he would go and see his invalid mother. "She read your books, and she wants to see you." Dr. Miller went to her, but when he saw he was in a Catholic home he did not offer to pray. Yet not only was he asked to lead in prayer; he was urged to return. This was the first of many calls there.

He did not wait to be urged to go to homes

outside of his own parish where he felt he might
be useful. Learning that a member of another
church, who lived near his own home, was an invalid, and knowing that her own pastor was unable to see her often, he called on her three times
a week for several years. " I am comparatively
well now," the recipient of these visits said a few
days after the close of Dr. Miller's earthly service, " and I feel that I owe my renewed health—
in large measure—to God's blessing on the regular
visits of that godly man. Oh, it was good to see
his kindly smiling face and to hear his words of
cheer and hope."

One morning a message came to the editorial
office telling of the death by accident of the little
daughter of a woman not a member of his church.
Dr. Miller took the next train and remained with
the mother until she was calm and serene.

Such visits made by some workers among the
members of another church might cause friction—
but never when Dr. Miller was the caller. His
spirit was so thoroughly understood and appre-
ciated that pastors of all denominations as well
as priests of the Catholic Church welcomed his
presence among their parishioners. They knew
that his life was ordered in accordance with the
plea once made by him in public:

" In the great central truths of Christianity all
evangelical churches are agreed. Let us not waste
a moment's time or a breath of energy in strife
with other believers; let us rather unite all our

energies in doing good, in honouring Christ by telling the story of His love to all men, and by carrying the joy and cheer of the gospel everywhere. The church that shows the world the most love, and that lives the most sweetly, the most joyously, the most helpfully, is the church that comes the nearest to the Master's thought. That is the sort of church that every Christian should strive to make his to be.''

The more numerous the demands on his time and attention and sympathy the better Dr. Miller was pleased. He was always thinking of others, and he liked to be '' spent clear out for others.'' His idea of the secret of happiness was given to one who asked him to compose a Christmas greeting to be sent to friends:

'' The less you think of what Christmas will bring to you and the more you think of what you can do for others, the happier will the day be. If you think of one who is not likely to receive any attention and plan to make the day bright for that one, joy will fill your own heart. This is the only secret.''

That this was his way of spending Christmas was learned by a friend who had been hoping to spend the holiday at home with his family. Christmas came on Sunday that year, and the friend had no engagements to preach. But on Saturday he was asked to preach in the morning for a pastor whose wife had just died, and in the evening for another pastor who was seriously ill. '' I won't say it is too bad you are to have a

Christmas like that,'' was Dr. Miller's comment.
'' You are not to be pitied, but to be congratulated. The best Christmas is a Christmas of
service. This morning at prayer I thanked God
for the busy week he has sent me. It has been
a glorious week. I have slept very little. The
burdens and woes of many have been on my heart.
There have been a number of special cases—some
that could be met by money, and some that money
could not reach. I rejoice that they have been
brought to me.''

Many of these cases were brought to his attention by visitors who came to the office. They came
singly and together, from morning to night, all
through the year. They were never denied ad-
mission, but were received by the secretary who
admitted them at once to Dr. Miller's room,—unless there was already a visitor there. The secretary's room frequently looked like the anteroom
of a famous specialist. It was a noticeable fact
that few of the waiting men and women spoke to
one another. Most of them were entire strangers.
They came from all parts of the city, from other
cities and states, and even from abroad. Frequently one came a long distance on purpose to
confer about some life problem that was troubling
him.

'' What tales those walls could tell,'' one of Dr.
Miller's friends once said, '' tales of tears, of
blighted lives, of discouraged parents, of ambitious youths, of anxious business men, of down-

hearted Christian workers, of penitent sinners! I wish I dared to tell a few of the incidents that I know, illustrating what has resulted from these short conferences. Aspiring young people are assisted to an education; the needy are tided over hard places; the transgressor is helped back to manhood and truth; homes are healed of dissensions that seemed fatal.''

What passed in that room was sacred. Dr. Miller did not betray the confidence of those who sought him. But sometimes circumstances made it necessary that one or two others should share a portion of the secret. For this reason it is possible to give a few glimpses into the lives of those who made pilgrimages to the room of this friend of Jesus.

A troubled woman told of her husband's difficulties. '' He is a splendid man,'' she said, '' but I know there is something preying on his mind. I cannot help him in this. I do not know who can, unless you will. He thinks everything of you, though you do not know him.'' So Dr. Miller went out in search of the husband, who held a position of trust with a large business house.

A stranger told the sad story of a husband and wife. The wife was employed in a store from which she brought home many things for which her husband knew they could not pay. '' You cannot afford this, can you? '' he would ask her. At last she was arrested for the theft of the goods, and he was arrested with her as a receiver of the stolen property. Before the case was called for trial the wife collapsed and was sent to the hospital. To the judge the husband stated the case, and appealed in behalf of the wife. "She will die if she goes to prison," he said. "I will plead guilty. Send me in her place." The prosecuting attorney agreed, and the judge sentenced him to serve eighteen months in jail. Verifying the facts as told him, Dr. Miller was able to secure the reduction of the term. Then the problem was to place the wife until her husband should be able to care for her. Learning that her mother lived in Boston, and that it would be possible for her to live with the mother and sew for a living, Dr. Miller arranged for this and paid the expenses to Boston.

With averted face a young woman told her story: She had been detected in shoplifting by an officer in one of Philadelphia's smaller department stores. When taken to the private office of a member of the firm, she confessed and asked for mercy. The business man told her she would be released on one condition—that she go to Dr. Miller, and tell him all about her sin, and listen to what he would say to her. And this man had no personal acquaintance with Dr. Miller, and was not a member of the church!

Two visitors from a town three or four hundred miles distant came to inquire for a boarding place within reach of St. Paul Church. "We have come down to spend the winter," the mother

said to Dr. Miller, " because my daughter needs
you. We have read your books, and we feel that
she should be able to listen to your preaching,
Sunday after Sunday. She is making a brave
effort to overcome a besetting sin. We feel that
you can help us as no other man can."

The telephone announced the arrival in the city
of two strangers who had hoped to reach the office
that afternoon. Their train had been delayed and
they wished to know if it was too late to call. Dr.
Miller was just leaving his office, so he asked them
to meet him at his home. There he spent half an
hour with them in sympathetic conversation about
their difficulties. After he had prayed with them,
they hurried away to catch a night train back to
the city from which they had come. They had
travelled many hours for the one purpose of talking with one who had already spoken to them
helpfully through his books!

A stranger explained that her husband of a
year had left her, and refused to return. Both
husband and wife were unknown to Dr. Miller, but
he went out at once, found the man, and persuaded
him to go home for a conference with his wife. He
himself went with the husband. For two hours
the three were together. When Dr. Miller left the
house the home which had been threatened with de-
struction was out of danger. From that day husband and wife dated the real beginning of their
happiness. Next day Dr. Miller wrote them a
long letter. Here are some paragraphs:

" You do not begin to understand my loving interest in you and your husband, and my desire for the complete restoration of the happiness of your home. It must not be possible for you two dear lovers to fall apart. Nothing really serious has happened to mar your fellowship. You have not understood each other quite perfectly—that is all —and you have not had quite patience enough with each other, so things have gone wrong a little, and your relations have become a bit tangled. But it is going to be all right now. You will not let anything so small do you both and your home such harm.

" Longfellow tells of going out one morning after a heavy night storm, and walking through his garden. Under a tree he saw a birds' nest lying on the ground. He pitied the birds, and stood there thinking sadly of their misfortune. But while he was musing, he heard a chattering overhead, and, looking up, saw the little birds busy building their nest again. They were not defeated nor greatly discouraged by the disaster.

" That is what I am sure you and your husband are doing already. The storm came and swept your nest to the ground. Yesterday it seemed to you that it could not be restored. But now you have taken time to think, and are bravely building the nest again. And it is going to be more beautiful, and fuller of love, joy and song than ever it has been before.

" It may not seem very easy to save your home after all that has happened, but no matter what it costs, it will be a thousand times worth doing. Love is the sweetest thing in the world, but love is not easy. It means much self-denial, much forgetting of one's own wishes, much restraining of one's own impulses, much curbing and check-

ing of one's own feelings. St. Paul tells us that
' love suffereth long, and is kind . . . doth not
behave itself unseemly, seeketh not its own, is
not provoked, taketh not account of evil; . . .
beareth all things, believeth all things, hopeth all
things, endureth all things.' It is not easy to love
in this way. It takes the grace of God in our
hearts to enable us to love after this fashion.

" You and your husband love each other. You
have not forgotten the lover days. When you
were first married, your love was deep and tender.
Somehow you have not always been happy since.
Little things have come in to make you unhappy
some days. But your love is really true and
strong as ever. It would break your hearts to be
separated. All you want is to get this love into
the common relations of your lives. You have not
quite learned yet how to deny yourselves and give
up for each other.

" There are wondrous possibilities in your married life. You two dear young people may be the
happiest in the city, and your home may become
the sweetest, happiest home in all the community.
All you need in order to realise these possibilities
is love worked out in thought, in word, in act, in
disposition. Do not blame each other when things
go awry—blame each, yourself. Never allow
yourself to be vexed or hurt, at least to show it,
no matter how much you think you have been
wronged, or how unjustly you think you have been
treated. Love each other as Christ loves you.
Repay unkindness with kindness. If you think
you have been unfairly treated, or unkindly, be
especially kind in return. That is the way to pay
back an evil thing done to you.

" God bless you. I believe that a year from
now you will tell me you have had the happiest

DR. J. R. MILLER (1904)

year you ever have had; that the nest which the storm tore down has been built again, and is more beautiful than ever it was before.''

The letter in full is given in the chapter '' Building Again the Home Nest '' in '' The Gate Beautiful.''

After reading of such experiences as these in dealing with the sorrows and anxieties of his visitors, no one will wonder that he gave this counsel to one who was perplexed:

'' With regard to yourself, let me say that the more implicitly you can trust Christ with your life and all its affairs, the sweeter will be your peace and the deeper the joy of your heart. It seems to me that people ofttimes miss blessing because they do not trust fully enough. God loves to have us trust Him. I know by experience the joy it gives to me to have some one repose implicit confidence in me, telling me everything. I often think that this must be a little hint of the joy which Christ has when we trust Him perfectly. We all know, too, how it pains us to have a friend withhold confidence, trust only partly, or perhaps fear and doubt us. This is also a suggestion of how Christ's heart must be grieved when we do not fully trust Him.''

One of those who unburdened his heart to this friend of the needy was a college student. In a letter written long after his graduation he told his own story:

'' I recall very vividly how, when I was at Princeton making my own way through college,

I was once very much disheartened and stopped in for a little heart-to-heart talk with you on my way back from my home. The kindness with which you talked my burden into blessing I shall not soon forget. That was in my freshman year. At that time you gave me a little book which I prize most highly. Afterwards you wrote to me a few times and I called in to see you on several occasions. All this, I presume, is forgotten by you. With me it is a sweet memory.''

One secret of Dr. Miller's Christlike living is laid bare in these paragraphs from his own pen:

'' I seek in the morning to give myself to my Master for that day, saying: ' Take me, Lord, and use me to-day as Thou wilt. I lay all my plans at Thy feet. Whatever work Thou hast for me to do, give it into my hands. If there are those Thou wouldst have me help in any way, send them to me or send me to them. Take my time and use it as Thou wilt.' I think no farther on than to-day, I make no attempt to give months and years to Christ. . . .

'' Sometimes the very first one to come to me in the golden hours of the morning, which are so precious to every student, is a book agent, or a man with fountain pens or stove polish, or perchance only a pious idler who has no errand but to pass an hour, or it may be one of those social news venders who like to be the first to retail the freshest gossip. Interrupted thus in the midst of some interesting and important work, my first impulse is to chafe and fret, but then I remember my morning consecration. Did I not put my plans and my time out of my own hands into my Master's? Let us beware that we do not bow out of our

door with a frown one whom God has sent either
with a message or a benediction for us; for even
in these prosaic days heaven sends angels, though
they may come unawares, not wearing their ce-
lestial robes, but disguised in unattractive garb.''

There was more to that morning prayer than
consecration. There was a period of earnest in-
tercession for people all over the world—people
who had written to him, or called on him, or whose
work he was following. One morning he turned
from such a prayer to pen a message to Dr. F. B.
Meyer in London:

'' I write a word which I hope may reach you
before you start on your Eastern preaching tour.
I cannot tell you what deep interest I have in
this journey of yours—this apostolic journey
which you are to make for the Master. I am sure
that God's blessing will be upon you. You will
have the prayers of thousands of friends as you
go your way to speak the words of Christ. Your
journey through this country left a path of blessing, and in eternity you will meet those who will
thank you for the words you spoke which made
the truth of Christ more clear and brought them
nearer to the Master's heart. I am sure that the
same blessing will attend you in your work in
India and elsewhere. Of course you will have the
difficulty of speaking through an interpreter, but
even this will not prove to be a serious hindrance,
when the Spirit of God speaks through you. I
write out of my heart just this word of farewell,
to assure you of prayer for you as you go upon
your mission. I trust that you will be preserved

in good health and will come back in due time refreshed and strong.''

The return of the mail brought grateful response from Dr. Meyer:

'' I am sure that your letter was prompted by the Spirit to strengthen me in view of this journey. Naturally my whole nature shrinks appalled and overwhelmed. But God says ' On.' And your letter is as a fresh assurance. I am full of preparation and work; so must be content with this. Only be sure that your words have been very sweet to me. What a comradeship there is on this battle field! What companionship when we get home! ''

Every morning he renewed his touch with Christ so that he would not lose it through the busy hours. It was his habit to close every day by reporting to his Friend. Of this habit he said:

'' The disciples returned at evening and made a report to Christ of their work. Thus I tell Him of my life during the day, my dealings with persons who have come into it, and whatever has been attempted—in short, the whole day's work: its efforts, failures, mistakes, sins and joys. That is my evening prayer.''

Evening prayer like that prepared him for the next day's consecration, so that each day's glimpse of his Friend was more satisfying and complete than that of the preceding day, and he was the more completely equipped than ever for his world-wide ministry of comfort and help.

VACATION DAYS

There is no doubt that, even in the estimation of men, talking of oneself does one harm, defeating the very end one has in view in seeking honour. It is almost universally true that whenever a man begins to talk about himself, he hurts himself with those to whom he speaks. He makes himself appear less noble and winning to them. The good things he says about himself, however true they may be, lose much of their lustre and worthiness by being proclaimed by his own lips. Self-praise never can appear lovely, no matter how true it is, nor how deserving. The spirit which prompts a man to talk about himself, however it may be disguised, is really self-conceit; and self-conceit is not only a disfiguring blemish in a character; it is also a mark of weakness in a life. Its revealing always makes one less strong and influential with one's fellows. Instead of taking the self-conceited man's own estimate of himself, people discount it so heavily that they are likely, on account of his self-praise, to rate him much below his true value. Thus a man's very object in talking about himself, and proclaiming his own virtues and good deeds, is defeated. He does not receive praise of men, but dislike and depreciation instead of praise.—*From " Talking About Oneself," in " Things to Live For."*

CHAPTER XII

VACATION DAYS

DR. MILLER was so busy ministering to others that he would seldom take time for a vacation. His pastoral work and his editorial duties were so pressing that the convenient season for vacation was usually just a little bit in the future. The thought of the sick who needed him and the homes from which some one might be called from earth held him in the city when the homes of many of his people were closed for a period; desire to give personal supervision to the editorial work committed to him by the Church kept him at his desk when his assistants were at the seaside or in the mountains.

Yet he never lost sympathy with others as they planned for vacation journeyings. It was not his way to insist that vacations were a foolish waste of time,—he urged others to take the rest they required, the reward of earnest toil, and the preparation for further toil, but when he was urged to take his own advice, his only reply would be a smile.

It was his delight to think of the pleasures of travel and the delights of the country for other people. But it never seemed to occur to him that these pleasures and delights were for him. It was enough for him that he could live on the memory of rambles in the fields and woods in past years. Such memories enabled him once to say to vacation wanderers:

" The vacation days furnish opportunity for reading a book which is not printed in ordinary type—the book of Nature. God wrote it himself. Every leaf is a little chapter, every flower teaches its sweet lesson, every blade of grass has its touch of inspiration, every waving tree is a whole volume in itself. Then mountains and rivers and valleys and seas are written all over the great thoughts of God. Blessed is he who learns to read what God has written in these natural things."

He used the vacation season as an opportunity to teach young people such lessons as these:

" One should not take a vacation from being good and doing good, even while resting. There is only one record of Jesus giving or seeking to give his disciples a vacation, and his word to them was not, ' Go ye apart, and rest awhile,' but ' Come ye apart, and rest.' They were to go with him. We are not to leave Christ and Christ's service or the Christ-life, when we turn aside for a little rest. Some people seem to think that they should drop everything, even their church life, sometimes their Christian behaviour, when they go away to take a vacation. But this is not right. We must be Christians wherever we go, for we are always on duty, we always represent Christ. Wherever we go we should go with Christ. Wherever we stay, even for a day, we should confess Christ."

Again he gave this word of kindly counsel:

"A vacation should be fruitful in wayside ministries of kindness. We lay down our routine duty and taskwork for a little while. We do not hurry away in the morning to school or office or field. We relax the tension and take life leisurely. But there is a work which we never should lay down— we should go on with love's duty just as diligently in our resting weeks as in our busiest days. Love is like God—it 'worketh hitherto,' it takes no vacations, knows no Sabbaths, never intermits. Love's ministry should go on while we are resting from business cares. Not always do people remember this, however. Some grow selfish when away from home and fail in those gentle courtesies and graceful services which are the charm of a truly beautiful life. Countless opportunities occur when we are travelling or tarrying at summer resorts for a ministry of gentle manners and thoughtful ways which leaves behind its unspeakable blessing. The things we do when we are not supposed to be doing anything, the thousand little unpurposed acts, are truer tests of the real character of our life than the things we do with purpose and intention."

On the rare occasions when he would go away from the city to seaside, to mountains, or to the home of a friend, his days might have been described most fittingly and accurately by those bits of counsel given to others. Always he was God's messenger of helpfulness and love. Wherever he was—on the hotel piazza, on the beach, on the forest pathway—others were eager to gather about him. When guests learned that he was in the house, as soon as possible they sought the author whose works they had read with delight, and when they talked with him they said to one another, " He is just like his books." He was in demand for morning prayer service in one hotel where he spent a week or two on several occasions, and on Sundays he was urged to preach. He was glad to respond to such invitations when this was at all possible, for preaching was a joy to him.

During the thirty-two years of his service as editor, he took but two real vacations. The first of these was in the spring of 1893. The Hon. John Wanamaker, his friend since the days of the pastorate at Bethany Church, was celebrating the close of his four years' service as Postmaster General in the cabinet of President Harrison by making a ten weeks' trip to Mexico and the Pacific Coast. Dr. Miller was urged to join the party, which was made up of the merchant's family and intimate friends. The busy editor felt that he could not think of such a long absence from his duties, but he finally consented to join the party, four weeks after leaving Philadelphia, at El Paso, Texas, at the conclusion of the Mexican tour.

At El Paso, where he spent Easter Sunday, the pastor of the Congregational Church took advantage of the opportunity to have Dr. Miller preach one of his tender Easter sermons. Dr. Miller's heart went out in sympathy to the lonely pastor whose nearest Presbyterian neighbour was two

hundred miles distant, and whose people were zeal-
ously working in their difficult field. This Sunday
service by the wayside was a prophecy of later
Sundays of the vacation—always such insistent
demands were made on the traveller that he forgot
weariness and spoke to people who heard his word
with gladness.

Next day Dr. Miller joined Mr. Wanamaker's
party in their private cars, and continued the journey to California. Every mile of the way was a
delight to him, as was shown by full letters to the
New York *Evangelist*. The busy pen was not permitted to be idle even one day.

Many paragraphs of these letters were devoted
to vivid descriptions of the scenery. But they
were composed in such a manner that a reader
familiar with the writer's devotional books would
have recognised his hand. For instance, who
could mistake this sentence:

" We all know how much genuine human interest adds to the enjoyment of any place or any
natural beauty. A visitor at a jeweller's looking
at an opal, remarked that it seemed dead and lus-
treless. The jeweller took it in his hand and held
it a few moments, and when he laid it down again,
it flashed with all the iridescence of the rainbow.
It needed the warmth of the human hand to bring
out its splendours. This country would seem to
need nothing to give full life to its scenery. One
might drive along through the streets and wander
through the canyons and climb the mountains and
breathe the wonderful air, and without receiving

a mark of hospitality or the touch of a human
hand he could not but be charmed. But when a
party is received into the home life and social life
as we were, a warm, rich glow is added to all
the loveliness of the place. The opal was made
to glow before our eyes with richest beauty by the
warmth of the hospitality we enjoyed.''

Again an illustration was used most happily in
connection with the narrative of natural beauty
made more than ever memorable by reason of the
loving greetings of friends of other days:

'' Love is never lost. Nothing that love does
is ever forgotten. Long, long afterwards the poet
found his song, from beginning to end, in the heart
of a friend. Love shall find some day every song
it has ever sung, sweetly treasured and singing
yet in the hearts into which it was breathed. It
is a pretty legend of the origin of the pearl which
says that a star fell into the sea, and a shellfish,
opening its mouth, received it, when the star became a pearl in the shell. The words of love's
greeting as we hurry by fall into our hearts, not
to be lost, but to become pearls and to stay there
forever.''

But the larger portion of each letter was given
to a discussion of the problems and progress of
the Presbyterian Church in particular and religion in general in the places visited. At Pasadena
he told of preaching for Dr. Fife at the Presbyterian church. From Oakland, California, he
wrote of a service in Dr. Coyle's church, and a
Sunday afternoon visit to Mills College, where

several hundred young women gathered to listen
to him. From San Francisco he described China-
town briefly, as if in a hurry to pass on to what
he evidently considered a far more important subject—the praise of consecrated men and women
who were giving their lives to take the gospel to
the transplanted heathen. Again from Tacoma
he wrote of holding a church service. At Salt
Lake City he preached one Sunday, and on Monday he excused himself when the party went to
visit a silver mine, that he might visit the Salt
Lake Collegiate Institute, speak to the pupils, and
meet the teachers. At Kansas City he preached
in the Second Church, and after service was
waited on by six students from Park College who
had walked the nine miles from Parkville to em-
phasise the letters of urgent invitation to visit
the college which he had been receiving for two
weeks. At seven o'clock Monday morning two
of the faculty and four of the students greeted
him and Mr. Wanamaker at the Kansas City
station and escorted them to the college town,
where they were met at the train by the entire
faculty and almost the entire student body. An
hour was spent at the chapel, where both visitors
talked.,

At the close of each service held along the way
there was an informal reception. Many people
wanted to say a word to Dr. Miller about his books,
and tell him how his words had helped them. As
always, he was astonished at the evidence of feel-

ing.   He acted as if he thought the words were meant for some one else.

In a letter to Mrs. Miller, written a few days before reaching Philadelphia, he told his delight in the unusual vacation:

" The tour has not been a mere vacation from work for Mr. Wanamaker and myself.   We have held services at every point.   I am sure that Mr. Wanamaker has left encouragement and new strength in hundreds of Christian hearts, especially by his words to Young Men's Christian Associations and Sunday-school teachers.   Certain it is that we would hardly have done as much preaching and speaking if we had been at home.   It has been almost like some of St. Paul's journeyings through the country to confirm the souls of the brethren.   This fact reconciles me to what on one side seems to me almost a waste of time in sight-seeing.   It does not look to me now as if the ' rest ' element had come to much, for I have not often been busier than on this journey.   I have a very heavy mail at every stopping place, and many local letters at every point, all of which must be answered.   Still I am no doubt getting rest in the change, and will come home fat and strong."

His last thought was not of himself, but of those whom he had met:

" It is to be hoped that we have left a little new cheer and courage in some earnest hearts along the way; certain it is that we have received blessing in our hearts and lives from the people we have met."

He returned from the six weeks' absence from his desk with humble heart:

" It ought to be worth a great deal to one to have had the opportunity of seeing all this natural beauty. It ought to make a better man of him, this beholding so much of the loveliness and grandeur God has made. It ought to make his heart gentler, his life purer and sweeter, his spirit more lovely. It ought to make him more reverent and exalted in all his thoughts and feelings. As we take up again our tasks and duties we shall all remember the happy days of privilege we have enjoyed and be the better for them."

Three years later, in the summer of 1895, Dr. and Mrs. Miller took their only real vacation trip together—six weeks in Europe. The outward-bound voyage gave Dr. Miller an unusual opportunity to greet a number whom he had known by name and through correspondence, but had never met. In a letter to the *Evangelist* he spoke of the presence of " several passengers whom everybody has wanted to meet, and whose influence has been stimulative of good fellowship and a cheerful, kindly spirit." It did not occur to him that he was one of the most sought for passengers in a company that included a number of famous men, or that his words about others aptly described himself.

A pleasant Sunday was spent in London. As usual, he was found in church, morning, afternoon and evening:

" For myself, I chose three preachers whom I wished to hear and sat through the full service in each place. In the morning, I visited the City Temple and listened with real interest and profit to Dr. Joseph Parker. The great building, which is said to seat 2,700 people, was filled from pulpit to door. The prayer was reverent, inclusive, tender, and full of sympathy. Although it was brief, yet nobody was left out. Dr. Parker announced no text, but spoke in general on charity in judging others. The sermon was full of excellent thoughts and suggestions. In the afternoon, I went to Westminster Abbey to hear Canon Gore. There is not much comfort in attending services in the Abbey, as it is almost impossible to hear unless one gets a seat well to the front; there is so much confusion caused by people coming and going. To-day the throng was great, many of our countrymen attending. In the evening, I went to hear the Rev. F. B. Meyer. He is a preacher of rare power, Scriptural and spiritual. Few other men in the world are reaching out so widely in beneficent influence as Dr. Meyer. His little books and tracts have gone wherever the English language is read, and have carried everywhere a holy program of divine love and grace. He is a prodigious worker, never resting, yet never seeming weary."

In Paris he was invited to speak by Charles Wagner. After the service an American came to him, and said:

" I came to hear Mr. Wagner, and I was disappointed when you got up to speak. But I shall always be glad I heard you. I remember only one thing you said, but this I shall never forget. I refer to your definition of religion; you said, ' To me religion means just one thing: Jesus and I are friends.' "

The days in Paris were thoroughly enjoyed, but it was not until Geneva was reached that Dr. Miller felt at home. The knowledge that he was in the city where John Calvin lived and wrought, and where he was buried, stimulated him.

" I took an early opportunity to visit the Cathedral where the great theologian used to preach. It is a plain, thirteenth-century building showing many marks of age and decay. Close by is the house in which Calvin lived. In the Plain-Palais Cemetery is his grave, although it is unidentified, as Calvin's express instruction was that no mark of any kind should be put upon his tomb to tell where his body rested. His grave needs no stone, no monument, for he is not dead. He lives wherever the reformed faith is held and the doctrines which bear his name are taught."

From Geneva the journey was continued by way of Pisa to Rome. It was not the season ordinarily considered favourable for a visit to the city by the Tiber, but Dr. Miller longed to see the scenes made forever memorable by the presence of St. Paul and the persecution of the early Christians. A Sunday was spent in the city, and the travellers joined a little company of twenty-five people who gathered at the American Protestant Episcopal Church for the only English service held in the city that day.

Naples, Pompeii, Florence, Venice and Milan were visited in turn. On two Sundays Roman Catholic Churches were sought, as no Protestant Church was to be found. But when Lucerne was reached, the opportunity to attend the service maintained by the Scotch Free Church was welcomed.

Then came a leisurely trip through Germany, by rail and Rhine steamer. Attention was called in a letter to the *Evangelist* to the many relics and shrines in the cathedrals along the way, with this added comment:

" We need not wish for such reputed relics in our country. Better, infinitely better, is the simple Christian life which is found in thousands of our churches. Far better is it to have the Holy Spirit abiding in our congregations and giving comfort, strength, joy, peace and love, than to have such shrines and treasures as they show us in many of these great churches and cathedrals, and not to have the divine Presence. It is better to have the true Christ with us than to possess any piece of the wood of the ' true cross,' even if this were possible."

Another pleasant company shared the homeward voyage. One and another of these was singled out for warm praise by the traveller who always saw the best in others and rejoiced to be able to tell of it. Of one shipmate he said:

" He was a genius for kindness, and few if any have missed receiving from him some word of cheer and encouragement during the voyage."

Probably that is exactly what the passenger of whom the words were written would have said of Dr. Miller.

But vacation was over, so the letter which told of the voyage concluded:

" With gratitude to God for what we have enjoyed, we turn with eagerness to the work that waits."

He lost no time in getting to the work that waited for him. From Naples he had written to his associates in the editorial office:

" I shall be in Philadelphia on August 26."

His train reached the city half an hour after noon. Before two o'clock he was seated at his desk, ready to begin the work of another long period without a vacation.

THE LAST YEARS

Some one says that the secret of a happy old age is a well-watched past. The secret of any to-day is a well-watched yesterday. And there is no better way to keep our days beautiful and free from memories that vex us afterwards than to tell Jesus every night all that we have said and done during the day.—*From " Making Our Report," in " A Heart Garden."*

By and by in even the best life we come to a door which opens into old age. Many are disposed to feel that this door can lead to nothing beautiful. We cannot go on with our former tireless energy, our crowded days, our great achievements, But there is altogether too much letting go, too much dropping of tasks, too much falling out of the pilgrim march, when old age comes on. We may not be able to run swiftly as before. We tire much more easily. But old age may be very beautiful and full of fruit. This door opens into a period of great possibilities of usefulness, a true crowning of the life. Old age is not a blot, if it is what it should be. It is not a withering of the life, but a ripening. It is not something to dread, but is the completion of God's plan.—*From " Life's Open Doors," in " The Book of Comfort."*

Death is not a period in the sentence of life—it is only a comma, a little breathing place, with more to come after. Just how the sentence after the comma will read, we cannot know. Just in what form we shall continue to live, we may not even guess. We know that we shall be the same persons. Individuality will never be lost. I shall be I through all changes and transformations. The being that shall be serving God a million years hence will be the same person that played about the home early in childhood, wrought in the hard tasks of mature days, and suffered and sorrowed. I will always be I—there never can be any confusion of individuality. This is perhaps all we can assert positively about the immortal life. But this is a great deal. We shall lose nothing in our efforts. This makes it immensely worth while to live.—*From " The Meaning of Immortality," in " The Book of Comfort."*

CHAPTER XIII

THE LAST YEARS

FOR years friends who looked on as Dr. Miller did the work of three men expressed the fear that he would break down long before he was seventy. As the years passed without the fulfillment of their prophecies they marvelled. They saw no appreciable difference in his strength until 1909, when he suffered a slight stroke of apoplexy. The effect of this seemed to pass off very soon, and for two years he was as active as ever, at his desk, in the homes of the people and in the pulpit. His physician urged him to spare himself—but he never knew what it meant to spare himself.

On his seventieth birthday his office was a bower of bloom, and his mail was burdened with greetings from those whom he had cheered and helped by his personal words, his articles, his books, his sermons. They welcomed the opportunity to tell him what his life had meant to them.

One of the first messages to reach him was this, from Rev. C. R. Blackall, D.D., Editor of Periodicals of the American Baptist Publication Society:

"You see that I have beaten you ten years in the life race, and feel my importance in dealing

with my junior brother. I send loving congratu-
lations. You don't belong to one church, or to
one denomination; you belong to all churches of
all denominations! Who ever heard the faintest
suggestion by you, with pen or voice, to crucify
or ostracise somebody who dared to speak or to
believe differently from yourself? You believe in
a square deal with your brethren; that is one reason why I love you so much. My love for you has
grown deeper and deeper as the years have rolled
on. God bless you. Your shadow will abide in
the years ahead when the Master calls you to
higher and more extended service with himself.''

A fellow editor made discriminating comment
on the wonderful work done through thirty years:

'' I have tried before to indicate to you my
amazement at the voluminousness and variety of
your wholesome and effective contributions to the
life of the Church. The amazement grows, and
with it thanksgiving to God. The nearest parallel
to this that I know of in modern times was Spur-
geon; and both in continuousness and in literary
charm and lasting quality, even his rare genius
seems to me outshone by your work; while also
you keep it up to a riper age. I have always
found rare pleasure and profit in perusing your
pages. I am sure your writings have gone deep
and far into the development of modern piety.
I like your sanity and sagacious reserve much,
as well as your delightful and potent simplicity
of expression; and the touching tenderness of
your own constant mood suffuses your work with
a glow from Galilee which wins, soothes and
strengthens. You seem to have an instinct for
phases of truth which appeal to the hunger of the

heart and survive the changes of our jostling time. I imagine that few or none of your sentences will need to be expunged or passed over with silent apology a hundred years from now. Moreover, what you say ministers to the organic development of the Kingdom, as well as to the needs of individuals. The combination is extremely rare. Did you ever read of ' the hand of steel in a velvet glove '? The surface of your work is always unruffled, its form never rugged, so far as I have been able to note; but one comes to feel and see the hard fibre beneath. Personally, and as a lover of the Kingdom, I thank God for your labours and your words, and for the bow that abides in strength beyond the threescore years and ten; may it so continue long! ''

From a distant state came this birthday letter:

'' Five years ago one ignorant virgin who did not realise that she had a lamp at all was helped by your interest, friendship and sympathy to hold her lamp up and let it be lighted from the great Light. The foggy, unhealthy atmosphere of doubt and unbelief were driven out and disclosed right near was the great Friend.''

One who had worked with Dr. Miller for a long time told us of the thoughts the anniversary brought to his mind:

'' What a tremendous sight it would be if all the millions of people who have been helped by you could gather in one company to give greeting to you as you enter on another decade of service! What messages they would send if they could speak! How they would tell of comfort received, of courage renewed, of inspiration given, of new visions of life, of glimpses of the Master—all through the life that God has so richly blessed during the nearly half a century of your ministry.

"I am glad that I, as one of this vast company, have the opportunity to tell you how I thank God for the association with you which has become one of the greatest joys of my life."

From the Board which he had served so long came this record of an action taken by a standing vote:

"In view of the fact that Rev. J. R. Miller, D.D., the Editorial Superintendent of the Board, has just passed his seventieth birthday, the committee desires to place upon its minutes an expression of its high appreciation of his character and services.

"For nearly thirty years he has been a most loyal and efficient helper in the work of the Board.

"Genial, tactful and courteous in his bearing, he has also been wise and able as an editor to a degree which has brought great distinction to himself and honour to the Board. Under his supervision and direction, the periodical publications of the Board have attained a standard of excellence which has not been surpassed, if it has been approached, by any similar publications.

"The committee desires to congratulate Dr. Miller that the passage of the years has not diminished his capacity for, or interest in, his work, and to utter the sincere hope and prayer that he may be long spared to maintain his present relation to the Board and the activities of the Church."

One of the Philadelphia morning papers printed conspicuously a letter from Rev. Frank De Witt Talmage, D.D., in which he said:

" I doubt if there is a living minister in all the world who has done a greater work, or who is more internationally known, than the Rev. J. R. Miller, of this city, who is celebrating his seventieth anniversary. In the ecclesiastical life he is the marvel of the age. He has done the work of ten men, and yet to-day he is working harder than ever.

" While others have been attending banquets or sitting by their firesides of an evening, his tireless feet have been tramping the streets of the city calling upon the sick and like Paul carrying the gospel into many homes.

" I do not think it is an exaggerated statement to make that his name is known farther and loved more than that of any other Philadelphian, be he lawyer, merchant, or minister. Of all the great ministers of the past not one has wielded greater influence for good. The whole city should be thankful for the noble life of this wonderful man."

Another Philadelphia daily said, editorially:

" This day marks Dr. Miller's attainment of the allotted three score years and ten after a life that has had few, if any, idle hours. . . . His is a record of service of which any man might well be honestly proud."

The anniversary was observed at St. Paul Church by a Sunday evening congregation of more than fifteen hundred people. In responding to

addresses made by Dr. Lee, the associate pastor
of the church, the Hon. John Wanamaker, Judge
Willson, President of the Presbyterian Board of
Publication, Dr. Miller said:

" I cannot trust myself to say anything to-
night. It must be some other man you are talking about. You don't mean me—you must mean
my congregation—not me. It is not what I have
done; it is what you have done. The letters and
the telegrams, so filled with love, have gladdened
my heart beyond all description. I thank God
that I have had a share in leading you in your
lives. It has been a great privilege. My one purpose is to fill the years so full of humble, loving
service that every birthday shall mark a year of
complete consecration to the Master. I feel as
Louis Kossuth said: ' I would like my life to re-
semble the dew, which falls so noiselessly through
the night, and just as silently passes away, soon
as the rays of the morning's sun beams upon the
earth. Unnoticed by men's eyes, save for an oc-
casional iridescent sparkle here and there upon
some blade of grass, it is drawn upward and
passes away—but all that it has touched is fresh-
ened and beautified by its silent yet potent presence.' "

Three months after the anniversary service Dr.
Miller had a second slight apoplectic stroke which
affected his entire right side. An associate in the
editorial office who found him sitting helpless at
his desk was greeted with a smile, and the words:

" It has come. It is all right."

This was the way he received what he thought was to prove the summons to his Friend.

But he was to be spared yet longer to minister to the world. He rallied, and in September was again in the office. He made one slight concession to failing strength—he reached his desk fifteen minutes later in the morning and left as much sooner in the evening, but even so he was at work before the arrival of any of his assistants, and remained for some time after the last of them went home. He still allowed himself only ten minutes for lunch, as in previous years. Sometimes he did not leave his desk for even this brief interval.

He continued to preach at St. Paul Church usually once a Sunday, to conduct the prayer meeting, and to make his visits of comfort and inspiration. Dr. Lee did all he could to relieve him of responsibility, but he wished to be of the utmost possible use to his people while strength was given him, so he would not give up his work.

The unusually warm days in July, 1911, were hard on him, and he was compelled to go to Atlantic City for the month of August. When he returned he had to make use of an invalid's chair from the car to the waiting cab. Yet he insisted on going from the railway station to his office.

During September and October he was unable to walk without assistance, but was at work every day and almost all day, using a cab morning and evening. In November he felt strong enough to use the street cars and to continue his visits in the homes of the people. Again his physician warned him that unusual exertion might cause death at any time, as the blood vessels were hardening, and the enlargement and dilatation of the heart were becoming more and more evident. While he tried to coöperate with the physician in relieving the conditions, he felt that he could not take the time to stop work and care for himself.

At length increasing feebleness led him to ask for the severing of the ties with the church which he had seen grow from nothing. Yet even then he could not forego the privilege of going to the sick room of some sufferer or kneeling with those from whom God had called a loved one. Sometimes it was necessary to use a cab for these visits, but he continued them as long as he could—and this was far longer than almost anyone else would have thought possible.

His seventy-second birthday found him still able to reach his desk and do effective work. Again there came to him scores of letters from all parts of the world which made him more eager even than before to work for others with his last ounce of strength.

Perhaps the most striking of the greetings on this anniversary was an editorial utterance in *The Christian Endeavour World:*

" You are still a young man, Dr. Miller, though you have advanced one day into your seventy-third year. You know the secrets of perpetual youth: love to God, love to man, and hard work. You are a Presbyterian, and no one has better served that great denomination than its editorial superintendent for more than three decades. But you are also a universal Christian leader. Millions of all denominations, in all lands, have read your sixty books, and have entered with you into the holy places. But in the Great Day, when your books and your faithful and brilliant editorial service are gratefully remembered, there will be for you a crown outshining these: the crown of the earnest pastor and the loving, sympathetic friend. And many thousands will press to join you in your coronation."

A little more than a month later Dr. Miller closed his desk for the last time. "His legs have been worn out in the service of St. Paul Church," his physician—one of the elders of the church—explained to inquiring friends.

But while his legs had given out, his brain was active. His days were spent in conferences with editorial associates, examining the editorial mail, dictating replies to important letters, receiving visits from those who came to him for counsel and help, and arranging and revising chapters for "The Book of Comfort" and the eighth and last volume of "Devotional Hours with the Bible."

Always he was cheerful and happy. There was no vain longing for the activities that he felt he would never again be able to take up, for always he was living in the spirit of words written to his anxious friends at the church:

" I understand that when I am physically unable to do the work I would be doing if I were able, it is not my work at all. It would have been mine if I were strong and well. But now my duty is just to rest and be still, and let others do the work which I cannot do. The Good Shepherd's call to me now is not to follow in the dusty way, but to ' lie down in green pastures.' Neither is the time of lying down lost time. Duty is not all activity. Sometimes it is to wait and sing. Nothing is going wrong in my life because I am not in what would be my place if I were well. My ministry is not broken or even interrupted by this experience. My work for my Master has not been stopped—its form only has been changed."

A chapter in " The Book of Comfort " which came in inspired fervour from his hands on one of the days when he was so feeble he could hardly hold the pen is entitled " When We Are Laid Aside." The closing sentences enforce the lesson as given earlier to his people:

" We may be laid aside from our active work; but God never lays us aside from Himself. So we need never lay aside our joyous witnessing for Him, His love and His keeping power. If that witness has counted for much when we were active, it can count for more in our inactivity. If we have wasted the days of our activities by failure to witness for Him, we may yet, in Christ's strength, start to-day, in our new helpfulness, upon a showing forth of God's presence in our life that shall gladden Him and change His world."

During the first weeks when Dr. Miller was witnessing for his Master by his ability to keep serene in inactivity, the General Assembly of the Presbyterian Church, in session at Louisville, Kentucky, did him unusual honour. Immediately after the adoption by the Assembly of the Resolutions of the Report of the Board of Publication and Sabbath School Work, Rev. J. A. Worden, D.D., took the platform and said:

" The Rev. J. R. Miller, D.D., Editorial Superintendent of the Board, is critically ill. Side by side he and I have laboured for thirty-two years. Now it is feared that Dr. Miller, whom so many thousands love for his own sake, is sick unto death. The hand that has written messages of Christ's truth and love to millions in this and other lands seems forever to have dropped the pen. The feet that went about Philadelphia's streets on errands of mercy, as those of few others have ever done, now appear to be finally paralysed by unwearied going. The voice that for fifty years preached and taught Christ publicly and from house to house, is almost still, and the heart that only throbbed for love of God and man is slowly ceasing to beat.

" May I have the privilege of moving that this General Assembly do now join in prayer for our beloved Dr. Miller—minister, writer, editor, counsellor, friend,—and that by a rising vote we send to Dr. Miller a message of prayer, sympathy and love? "

The resolution was adopted by a rising vote, and the Assembly was led in prayer. Later Rev.

W. H. Roberts, D.D., the Stated Clerk, sent this message to Dr. Miller:

" It is my privilege to communicate to you the action of the General Assembly, expressing its sympathy with you in your serious illness. The fact of your illness was presented to the Assembly by the Rev. James A. Worden, D.D., Commissioner from the Presbytery of Philadelphia, and immediately after the adoption of the Report of the Assembly's Standing Committee on Publication and Sabbath School Work. After Dr. Worden's appropriate and touching address, the Assembly was led in prayer, and in a most felicitous manner, by the Rev. M. A. Brownson, D.D., pastor of the Tenth Presbyterian Church, Philadelphia. It is proper to add that the Assembly, generally and individually, realised the great value of your services to the Church through many years, and cherished the hope that you would, in due time, be restored to that field of labour which you have made so fruitful for the glory of Christ and the welfare of souls."

To this letter Dr. Miller sent the characteristic response:

" I am deeply grateful for the Assembly's message. The kind words sent from all over the world tell me that the end of my work is at hand. I am ready."

Increasing feebleness kept the invalid in bed during the last weeks of June. He suffered little. For a time he knew those who stood by his bedside, but during the last few days his mind wandered

and the light of recognition was seldom in his
eyes. But the light that is not of earth was becoming more and more noticeable to those who
had the privilege of looking on his smiling, happy
face.

He had already passed beyond the reach of
such words as these that came from Dr. F. B.
Meyer:

" I hear that my beloved friend is very near
his Home-Going. If he is able to hear of any
human friend whom he has loved, please mention
my name to him; tell him that I have loved him
and that his love has been sweet. Ask him to look
out for me when I come."

The end of life on earth came without warning
on the afternoon of July 2, 1912. Mrs. Miller and
the only daughter, Mary Wanamaker Miller
(Mrs. W. B. Mount), were present, but it was
impossible to summon the sons—William King
Miller and Russell King Miller. One moment Dr.
Miller seemed to be resting quietly; the next he
was at rest.

He had gone to be with his Friend. For him
the new life had begun—the life of which he delighted to speak as " a clause in the sentence of
existence, begun after the comma which we call
death."

" Oh, how happy Jesus must be now! " was the
glad comment made by one of the little grand-
children who had delighted to romp with him whom
God had called to Himself.

The funeral services, held in St. Paul Church, were most simple. They were arranged according to Dr. Miller's wishes made known months before to members of the family and to Dr. Lee. There was no address, but only prayer, the reading of Scripture, the repeating of the Twenty-third Psalm by the vast congregation, the singing by a soloist of " He will lead His flock like a Shepherd " from Handel's " Messiah," and the singing by the congregation of Dr. Miller's favourite hymn:

> " O Love that wilt not let me go,
>   I rest my weary soul in Thee;
> I give Thee back the life I owe,
> That in Thine ocean depths its flow
>   May richer, fuller be.
>
> " O Light that followest all my way,
>   I yield my flickering torch to Thee;
> My heart restores its borrowed ray,
> That in Thy sunshine's blaze its day
>   May brighter, fairer be.
>
> " O Joy that seekest me through pain,
>   I cannot close my heart to Thee;
> I trace the rainbow through the rain,
> And feel the promise is not vain
>   That morn shall tearless be.
>
> " O Cross that liftest up my head,
>   I dare not ask to fly from Thee;
> I lay in dust life's glory dead,
> And from the ground there blossoms red
>   Life that shall endless be."

TRIBUTES OF AFFECTION

Not one of us ever dreams of all the possibilities of his life. The plainest of us carries concealed splendours within him. If we knew what noble qualities are lying undeveloped within us, what powers are waiting to be called out, what few things we may achieve in the years before us, it ought to inspire us to our best life and effort. Perhaps no one ever does reach in this world all that he might attain.—*From " The Awakening of Life's Glory," in " A Heart Garden."*

Most people employ but a fragment of the capacity of their life and then allow great measure of capacity to lie undeveloped, and in the end to atrophy. A volume could be filled with a description of a human hand, its wonderful structure, and the things it can be trained to do. Yet how many hands ever reach the limit of their possible achievements? Think of the powers folded up in a human brain and of the little of these powers most of us ever bring out in life. Now and then a man starts in ignorance and poverty and reaches a greatness in ability and in achievement which amazes the world. Doubtless thousands and thousands who never attain anything beyond mediocrity have just as great natural capacity, but the splendid powers of their life are allowed to run to waste. They are lacking in energy and do only a little of what they might do.—*From " In That Which Is Least," in " The Book of Comfort."*

CHAPTER XIV

TRIBUTES OF AFFECTION

WHILE it was Dr. Miller's request that no flowers be laid on the casket and that no words of eulogy be spoken at the funeral service, he could do nothing to prevent the writing of tributes to his memory by editors and correspondents everywhere.

As soon as the telegraph spread the news that he had gone to live with his Friend letters began to come in an avalanche. Within a week or two memorial services were held in churches in different parts of the country—not only churches where he was known personally, but churches where no one could tell of him except as they had learned to value him because of his letters, his work as editor, and his books.

Among the hundreds of letters which told of gratitude to God for his life and related instances of his helpfulness three may well find place here, as they represent well the spirit of all the correspondents.

A Philadelphia pastor who had known him for many years said:

" I was a lad when Dr. Miller came to Bethany and have been honoured with his friendship ever

since. I know of no man in the ministry of our
Church who has been so varied and abundant in
his work, and whom God so richly and manifestly
blessed in every department of his work.   His
editorial and literary work has had a world-wide
fame, and deservedly so. The effect of whatever
he wrote, whether in the form of tract, magazine,
or book, was edifying and comforting. His writing resulted in character-building on the one hand,
and the building up of broken hearts on the other.
Eternity alone can reveal the extent of the cheer,
the encouragement, the inspiration and the comfort which he produced by personal word or by his
pen.

"Our own home in very recent days has been
blessed with his words of comfort in the time of
sore bereavement and deep sorrow. He was truly
a ' son of consolation.'

"But Dr. Miller not only had a great heart,
he had also a great mind. Generations yet to
come will acknowledge this as his editorial and
literary work are more leisurely reviewed. It is
acknowledged everywhere now, but his reputation
in this regard will be much wider later on."

Messrs. Hodder and Stoughton, through whom
Dr. Miller's books found their way to the homes
of Great Britain and her colonies, wrote to Mrs.
Miller:

"As friend and as author Dr. Miller meant
very much to us and we deplore his loss more
than we can possibly say. We look back on the
long years of our relationship with the feeling of
bitter pain that they are closed, and great thank-
fulness for all the kindness, the consideration, the

affection that have made them forever memorable in our firm's history. We have lost a dear friend, as well as a very valued and most esteemed author. And we are very sorrowful. . . . There are so many to whom his name is forever blessed. Of him, more than of most, it is true that his works do follow him. He still speaks, and will ever speak, while there are worried, troubled hearts to listen.''

Rev. Herrick Johnson, D.D., LL.D., who was a pastor in Philadelphia during Dr. Miller's early years at Bethany, paid this tribute:

'' He was one of the noble company that I knew here in Philadelphia in very blessed association when I was here as pastor of the First Church. We all loved him. His place in our ministerial circle was unique. His gentleness made him great. His winsomeness had no weakness in it. Yet somehow everybody felt drawn to him. He seemed so closely in touch with the best in heart and life. Gentle as a child, yet firm as a rock, genial in spirit, lovable, helpful, always true, always tender, the memory of him is a benediction.''

The editor of *The Continent* called him '' A Twentieth Century Saint,'' and said:

'' No man identified with the Presbyterian Church in America has ever been more profoundly or more widely loved than Dr. James Russell Miller, the Editorial Superintendent of the denominational Board of Publication—just now ' gone on before.' And well did he deserve love. In him the gentleness of manhood and the manhood of gentleness combined to make the simple life of an unmistakable modern saint—a saint of the Christ sort, attaining holiness not in ascetic withdrawal from the world nor in pretentious piety exhibited for admiration of the world, but in day-by-day service humbly rendered for the weal of just as much of the world as he could bring within his patient and laborious reach.

" It was in the beautiful church home of the latter congregation that Dr. Miller's friends paid to him marvellous memorial tribute of love. The services were of the simplest sort because Dr. Miller had so commanded that they must be. Just before his death he had even forbidden that flowers should be heaped upon his coffin. But the richer and lovelier flowers of a tender reverence from hosts of friends acknowledging his helpfulness bloomed around his bier, and the whole atmosphere of the church, which owed its very existence to his fidelity, was electric with spoken and unspoken tributes to the glorious success of a life that sought no other wealth than the wealth of a great opportunity to serve."

In *The Presbyterian Banner*—published in the city where Dr. Miller secured his seminary training—was this strong message:

" Dr. Miller was an acceptable preacher and winsome pastor, as was shown in the way time and again a handful of people gathered up by himself grew to a great congregation. But his chief gift and work was as a writer. As editor of our Sunday-school periodicals he was pouring into their pages a steady stream of articles and comments, and these from time to time were gath-

ered up into books. He was an astonishingly pro-
lific writer, and produced no fewer than sixty
volumes. These were nearly all expository and
devotional in substance and style and have fed a
whole generation on their appetising and wholesome bread. He had a genius for seeing the homi-
letical uses of things, and every common thing or
daily event or experience became a text in his
hand for a practical application and interesting
bit of preaching. His writings . . . are wonder-
fully tender and beautiful. If there are few thun-
der clouds and lightning flashes, raging torrents
and cataracts in his pages, they are full of summer
peace and beauty, everywhere flushed with little
rivulets that keep the grass green and besprinkle
it with flowers. His books are restful and soothing, full of quiet but fresh inspiration and cheery
optimism, and they have comforted and encouraged countless thousands of readers. The whole
Church will mourn and miss him, and his loss will
be felt far beyond our bounds.''

This editorial word in *The United Presbyterian*
revealed the affection inspired by Dr. Miller in
the denomination from which he sought release in
1868:

'' Dr. Miller was one of those men whom no denomination can monopolise. His ambition to do
good was as wide as the longings of the human
heart. He belonged emphatically to the Church of
Christ. All denominations found in his literature
help and comfort and blessing; all firesides felt the
glow of his own warm heart. He was no contro-
versialist, but one who desired to bring the peace
of God to sorrowing souls. Quiet, unobtrusive,

unassuming in his life, out of his own experience and hope he gave his message to humanity. He spoke to the soul of all men, and they are few, if any, who have read his writings, but have been made better by them. His influence is not entombed with his body, but lingers, as the youth of the springtime or the summer sunshine, to continue year after year in the homes and hearts of the generations that follow. When his kindly features are forgotten, when the friends who knew and loved him have passed from earth and slumber with him in the dust, the words that he has written will be his memorial to their sons and daughters. We cannot estimate the influence of such a life. It is mightier than warrior's or statesman's. It is like the life of Jesus Christ in that its purpose is to make men better, purer, richer in riches that perish not, and wise in the wisdom that never faileth.''

The Sunday School Times—whose editorial columns Dr. Miller enriched by scores of articles which later became chapters in his books—said:

'' To serve the commonest needs of the many calls for a very uncommon man—he does it best in whom Christ shines forth most clearly. And Christ was the secret of the utterly unusual service to everyday men and women which Dr. J. R. Miller rendered through the long and fruitful lifetime which has now ceased in the flesh, to be glorified in richer measure beyond. Dr. Miller's mission in writing seemed to be to give out the simple things of God for which a hundred thousand hearts were hungering. His spirit was always childlike; therefore he could help many. And his writings had the rare quality of universal service because his personal life was ceaselessly serving in the same way. His individual ministries of love to men and women about him were indefatigable. His life was one of the most remarkable, in its high-pressure efficiency and output, of our generation. As author, editor, pastor and friend, he seemed to accomplish all the time about twice as much as most men, and never be hurried or strained as he did it. His life was a challenge and a benediction, a rebuke and comfort, to those who knew him well. The Saviour who was his life showed himself forth marvellously through Dr. Miller, as He will through anyone who is as eager as Dr. Miller was to let Christ live in him and serve through him.''

The editor of *The Christian Endeavour World* thus told his readers of the passing from earth of one whom he had been proud to number among his contributors:

'' The death of few Americans will be more mourned than that of Rev. J. R. Miller.

'' In spite of his enormous literary and editorial work Dr. Miller was always an enthusiastic and abundantly successful preacher and pastor, and has told the writer more than once that he would rather give up all his other work than this.

'' Dr. Miller's books . . . combine a rare sympathy with humanity, a deep appreciation of all that is best in literature, and a sturdy common sense that renders every line he ever wrote stanch and strong.

'' Even more than any of these aspects of his life, those who knew Dr. Miller will cherish the memory of his personal character; it was so sweet, so strong, so true to the best ideals. A man of tireless industry, he always had time to do the little kindly acts that make up so much of the happiness of this world; and many thousands— probably many more thousands than he himself ever guessed—will rise up at the last day and call him blessed.''

One of the Philadelphia daily papers—the *Public Ledger*—gave place in its editorial columns to a communication from the pastor of a Methodist Episcopal Church:

'' A few years since, while occupying the same seat with Dr. Miller on our way to New York City, I came to get a glimpse of his inner life that deepened all my former impressions of the man. While conversing on local matters pertaining to our respective denominations, I asked him to tell me in a single word what was the requirement that he, a man then seventy years of age, felt was needed especially to-day to be emphasised by the Christian ministry—Roman Catholic as well as Protestant.

'' After a moment of thought, as his eyes glanced over the rippling waters of the Delaware River which we were passing, he earnestly replied, ' Sincerity.'

'' That word marked the keynote of his own life in public and private. He was a sincere worshipper of his Lord and Master and consequently a sincere friend to all whom he met. His capacity for turning off work and for accomplishing things worth while surpassed that of any man of his years of my acquaintance.''

The readers of *The Congregationalist* were told of Dr. Miller's home-going in this paragraph:

" Dr. Miller was a teacher, a worker and a saint. His prodigious and untiring labours in various fields of industry bore abundant and lasting fruit. He had the rare gift of keeping many irons in the fire at once and keeping them warm. We have been in his office in the Witherspoon Building when he was constantly interrupted not only by his own office workers but by members of the large parish which he was serving. And, notwithstanding this constant outgo of sympathy and counsel and this exercise of control, Dr. Miller was as serene and quiet as befits one's conception of the author of books that have carried strength and comfort to many a needy heart. He not only did his editorial work well, but carried along with it the responsibility for several strong Philadelphia churches which he served in succession, devoting his evenings to parish visiting and his Sundays to preaching. No man could have thus successfully combined several important functions without loving every side of his work and without keeping in constant communication with the Source of spiritual power. We are among the multitude who loved and revered Dr. Miller and who will miss him now that his work is ended."

Sir W. Robertson Nicoll paid his tribute in the columns of *The British Weekly:*

" Dr. Miller of Philadelphia, who may be justly called the most popular religious writer of his time, has passed away. There never, we should suppose, was a man who worked harder. He was

Editorial Superintendent of the Presbyterian Board of Publication, and his duties in this connection might well have absorbed his whole time and strength, for he had to supervise all the Sunday-school literature and all the books put forth by the Board, and these were many. In addition, he was himself a voluminous author. In the United States and in this country these books have literally sold by the million, and they have been translated into many languages. But Dr. Miller was not content with these achievements. He continued to be a Christian pastor, and he had built up in succession three prosperous congregations. . . . We need not characterise his writings; they are tender, winning and consoling, and have moved many to more faithful labour and more patient endurance.''

Rev. John T. McFarland, D.D., editor of the Sunday-school periodicals of the Methodist Episcopal Church, was in hearty accord with these expressions. He said:

" During the last eight years of his life it was my privilege to know Dr. Miller as a brother editor of Sunday-school literature, and during several of these years, on account of the close coöperation of our offices on special work, I was intimately associated with him. I always found him thoroughly fraternal in his spirit, always anxious to work in harmony with others, generously considerate of their wishes, and rejoicing always to find that in the essentials of faith and in the aims of Christian effort, the various denominations are so nearly in accord. The Sunday-school literature of his church, of which he had charge for so many years, was brought by him to a very high standard of excellence; and it was an evidence of the mental vitality and freshness which he maintained to the last that he was in keen sympathy with the advance movements in the field of religious education. He was absolutely loyal to the fundamentals of evangelical faith, but was open-minded to the latest knowledge of the Bible. He was a great teacher, a tireless worker, a Christian minister utterly consecrated to the service of his divine Master, devoting to that service his undivided time and strength.''

Rev. C. R. Blackall, D.D., for many years editor of the Sunday-school publications of the Baptist Church—a man ten years Dr. Miller's senior, and in active service at the time—wrote his impressions for *The Superintendent:*

'' There passed into rest on the second day of July last one of the most helpful and loving men I have ever known. Estimates of character and worth and work, to be fair, must be based very largely upon the hidden purposes of life, which unconsciously reveal themselves like bands upon a coat sleeve to any careful observer, and really show deep-seated principles of action.

'' Dr. Miller was not a theologian, and therefore was not controversial in thought or action; nor was he aggressive in dealing with practical questions of the day as related to Sunday-school methods and work. I had the pleasure and the honour of a close and unbroken friendship with him through a long series of years. We often discussed questions of deepest and mutual interest. I invariably found him both frank and responsive.

I sometimes thought him too timid; I know better now, and that he shrank from anything that could hurt, even with the tenderness of a noble and pure woman.

" As editor and writer he will always be best known, the world over, for his true and unvarying helpfulness. He evidently believed that a true life is worth more to the world than a knotty disputation; that Sunday-school teachers gain better spiritual results by best use of the great truths that lie upon the surface, and the honest application of these to the daily life; and this thought he faithfully and undeviatingly followed in his voluminous editorial articles and books.

" I loved him much. I shall surely meet him again, after the limitations of the flesh are forever overcome.''

Dr. Robert E. Speer, one of the Secretaries of the Presbyterian Board of Foreign Missions, wrote this heartfelt tribute:

" He was an irrefutable evidence of the truth of Christianity. No other religion and no other power could have produced such a type. Free from all religiosity with nothing in his dress or manner or vocabulary to indicate the preacher or religious teacher, he was yet one of the most indefatigable of personal Christian workers and one of the most devoted and wide-eyed comforters and prophets of our day. He did the work of three ordinary men with no haste and apparently with unlimited time to give to individuals. He was the best known and most widely read writer of devotional books in the world, but all of human life was of interest to him and he lived in practical affairs. For truth, genuineness, simplicity, accomplishing power, kind but discerning knowledge of men, considerateness, thoughtfulness in detail, range, definiteness and love it would be hard to find his equal. Measured against his world-wide and penetrating ministry the great and noisy political careers of the day seem paltry. He was a man of the abiding world who therefore was able to mould the world that does not abide. Thousands of lives look back to him with love and with personal evidence of his wonderful sympathy and friendship and wisdom.''

Professor W. Brenton Greene, D.D., of Princeton Theological Seminary, after twenty-five years of intimate association with him, said reverently:

'' If I dared let any man embody my idea of our Lord, I should find myself unconsciously turning to Dr. Miller for such embodiment. We can try to follow him only afar off, but it is one of God's best gifts to us that we have been given such an example of Christlikeness.''

In 1909—in the chapter on the death of Moses, as printed in the second volume of '' Devotional Hours with the Bible ''—Dr. Miller said:

'' Let us seek to make our lives immortal, not in shafts and monuments, not in riches and earthly honours, but by making the world better, by putting touches of beauty into other lives, by teaching and blessing little children, by encouraging the weary and disheartened, and by comforting human sorrow. Then we shall need no grave, with its

marble memorial, to keep our name alive. We
shall live in the things we have done.''

So Dr. Miller lives on the earth to-day, and will
live while the earth stands. For though his name
may in time be forgotten, the work that God enabled him to do will never perish.

BOOKS BY DR. MILLER

(In Order of Publication)

Week Day Religion, 1880.
Home Making, 1882.
In His Steps, 1885.
The Wedded Life, 1886.
Silent Times, 1886.
Come Ye Apart, 1887.
The Marriage Altar, 1888.
Practical Religion, 1888.
Bits of Pasture, 1890.
Making the Most of Life, 1891.
The Everyday of Life, 1892.
Girls: Faults and Ideals, 1892.
Young Men: Faults and Ideals, 1893.
Glimpses Through Life's Windows, 1893.
The Building of Character, 1894.
Secrets of Happy Home Life, 1894.
Life's Byways and Waysides, 1895.
For a Busy Day, 1895.
Year Book, 1895.
Family Prayers, 1895.
The Hidden Life, 1895.
The Blessing of Cheerfulness, 1896.
Things to Live For, 1896.
Story of a Busy Life, 1896.
A Gentle Heart, 1896.
Personal Friendships of Jesus, 1897.
By the Still Waters, 1897.
The Secret of Gladness, 1898.

The Joy of Service, 1898.
The Master's Blesseds, 1898.
Young People's Problems, 1898.
Unto the Hill, 1899.
Strength and Beauty, 1899.
The Golden Gate of Prayer, 1900.
Loving My Neighbour, 1900.
The Ministry of Comfort, 1901.
Summer Gathering, 1901.
How? When? Where?, 1901.
The Upper Currents, 1902.
To-day and To-morrow, 1902.
In Perfect Peace, 1902.
The Lesson of Love, 1903.
The Face of the Master, 1903.
Our New Eden, 1904.
Finding the Way, 1904.
The Inner Life, 1904.
Manual for Communicant Classes, 1905.
The Beauty of Kindness, 1905.
When the Song Begins, 1905.
The Best Things, 1907.
Glimpses of the Heavenly Life, 1907.
Morning Thoughts for Every Day in the Year, 1907.
Evening Thoughts, 1908.
The Gate Beautiful, 1909.
The Master's Friendships, 1909.
The Beauty of Every Day, 1910.
The Beauty of Self-control, 1911.
Learning to Love, 1911.
The Book of Comfort, 1912.
The Joy of the Lord, 1912.
Devotional Hours with the Bible, eight volumes, 1909-1913.

Other SGCB Classic Reprints

Solid Ground is honored to present the following titles, many for the first time in more than a century:

COLLECTED WORKS of James Henley Thornwell (4 vols.)
CALVINISM IN HISTORY *by Nathaniel S. McFetridge*
OPENING SCRIPTURE: *Hermeneutical Manual by Patrick Fairbairn*
THE ASSURANCE OF FAITH *by Louis Berkhof*
THE PASTOR IN THE SICK ROOM *by John D. Wells*
THE BUNYAN OF BROOKLYN: *Life & Sermons of I.S. Spencer*
THE NATIONAL PREACHER: *Sermons from 2nd Great Awakening*
THE POOR MAN'S OT COMMENTARY *by Robert Hawker* (6 vols)
THE POOR MAN'S NT COMMENTARY *by Robert Hawker* (3 vols)
FIRST THINGS: *First Lessons God Taught Mankind Gardiner Spring*
BIBLICAL & THEOLOGICAL STUDIES *by 1912 Faculty of Princeton*
THE POWER OF GOD UNTO SALVATION *by B.B. Warfield*
THE LORD OF GLORY *by B.B. Warfield*
A GENTLEMAN & A SCHOLAR: *Memoir of J.P. Boyce by J. Broadus*
SERMONS TO THE NATURAL MAN *by W.G.T. Shedd*
SERMONS TO THE SPIRITUAL MAN *by W.G.T. Shedd*
HOMILETICS AND PASTORAL THEOLOGY *by W.G.T. Shedd*
A PASTOR'S SKETCHES 1 & 2 *by Ichabod S. Spencer*
THE PREACHER AND HIS MODELS *by James Stalker*
IMAGO CHRISTI *by James Stalker*
A HISTORY OF PREACHING *by Edwin C. Dargan*
LECTURES ON THE HISTORY OF PREACHING *by J. A. Broadus*
THE SCOTTISH PULPIT *by William Taylor*
THE SHORTER CATECHISM ILLUSTRATED *by John Whitecross*
THE CHURCH MEMBER'S GUIDE *by John Angell James*
THE SUNDAY SCHOOL TEACHER'S GUIDE *by John A. James*
CHRIST IN SONG: *Hymns of Immanuel from All Ages by Philip Schaff*
COME YE APART: *Daily Words from the Four Gospels by J.R. Miller*
DEVOTIONAL LIFE OF THE S.S. TEACHER *by J.R. Miller*

Call us Toll Free at 1-877-666-9469
Send us an e-mail at sgcb@charter.net
Visit us on line at solid-ground-books.com

Uncovering Buried Treasure to the Glory of God

www.ingramcontent.com/pod-product-compliance
Lightning Source LLC
Chambersburg PA
CBHW022119080426
42734CB00006B/182